GETTING BACK UP AGAIN

IN MEMORY OF

Detective Senior Constable (retired)

Trevor 'Trev' Ernest Walter

26 March 1958–24 March 2024

Through selfless dedication to the care and service of others, and by always looking for the next big adventure, Trev, my friend, yours truly was . . . a life well lived.

HASTEN THE DAWN

GETTING BACK UP AGAIN

A plan to get your head back in the game

CRAIG SEMPLE

echo
PUBLISHING

Echo Publishing
An imprint of Bonnier Books UK
6/69 Carlton Crescent
Summer Hill NSW 2130
www.echopublishing.com.au

Bonnier Books UK
4th Floor, Victoria House,
Bloomsbury Square
London WC1B 4DA
www.bonnierbooks.co.uk

Echo Publishing acknowledges the traditional custodians of Country throughout Australia. We recognise their continuing connection to land, sea and waters. We pay our respects to Elders past and present.

First published 2024

Printed and bound in Australia by Griffin Press

The paper this book is printed on is certified against the Forest Stewardship Council® Standards. Griffin Press holds FSC® chain of custody certification SGS-COC-001185. FSC® promotes environmentally responsible, socially beneficial and economically viable management of the world's forests.

Editor: Simone Ford
Page design and typesetting: transformer.com.au
Cover design and illustration: Design by Committee

A catalogue entry for this book is available from the National Library of Australia

ISBN: 9781760687953 (paperback)
ISBN: 9781760687960 (ebook)

echo_publishing
echopublishingaustralia
echopublishing

ABOUT THE AUTHOR

Craig Semple was a career detective in the New South Wales Police Force for twenty-five years, investigating outlaw motorcycle gangs, homicides and hundreds of other serious crimes. Medically retired from law enforcement in 2013 due to psychological injuries, Craig is now a sought-after keynote speaker and mental health advocate.

Craig is the founding director of Mentality Plus, through which he has developed and delivered mental health, wellbeing and resilience education to thousands of people all over Australia. He is also an ambassador for the Black Dog Institute. Craig's first book, *The Cop Who Fell to Earth*, was published by Echo Publishing in 2023.

Also by Craig Semple

The Cop Who Fell to Earth

Contents

INTRODUCTION

Mental health problems are common

The most recent National Study of Mental Health and Wellbeing found that in the period 2020–21, close to half (43.7 percent) of the Australian population between the ages of sixteen and eighty-five had experienced a mental disorder in their lifetime (Australian Bureau of Statistics). That means they had symptoms of enough severity and duration to receive a diagnosis. These figures are comparable to other western countries, including the United Kingdom and the United States.

This statistic is important because even if we think we're bulletproof, like I once thought I was, given nearly one in every two of us will experience mental health problems, we shouldn't take our own mental health for granted. We should make our mental health and wellbeing a lifetime priority.

It is also an important statistic because even if we avoid experiencing problems with our own mental health, it is almost certain that someone we care about will, whether that be a friend, a work colleague or a family member. So the more aware and educated we are, the better prepared we will be to support those we care about when they need us.

And it is an important statistic to remember for those living with mental health problems. You are not alone. We don't usually feel shame or embarrassment from having a cold or a broken bone, and nor should we when having problems with mental health. And like a cold or a broken bone, for most, mental health recovery outcomes are possible.

But for many, recovery is made more difficult with the absence of some or all of the required elements: effective professional help tailored to the individual, solid support networks of family and friends, personal responsibility and commitment to action, and, most important of all, hope and belief.

I have written this book as a resource for both those living with mental health problems and those who care for them. It is intended to be a guide to setting up those elements of a good recovery framework. I am not a doctor, psychiatrist, psychologist, psychotherapist, counsellor or health professional of any kind. I have not, therefore, written this book from a medical viewpoint. I have primarily written this book from the viewpoint of a consumer, from my *lived experience* and the shared lived experience of countless others I have met and worked with. The voice of lived experience regarding mental health was for too long largely overlooked in literature, academic research and the wider community. Thankfully, with the gradual breakdown of the stigma surrounding mental health, the voice of lived experience is being noticed and even sought. There is so much we can learn in life from listening to the lived experiences of others, and this is especially so regarding mental health and wellbeing.

In my first book, *The Cop Who Fell to Earth*, I shared the story of my twenty-five-year career in law enforcement, and that story needs little repeating here. The story I intend to share now is my subsequent journey through mental illness and recovery, but in much more detail than before and with the benefit of the knowledge I have acquired during my continuing career as a mental health educator. My intentions in doing so are multilayered, but they include a desire to: *break down the stigma* surrounding mental health; encourage *early help-seeking behaviours*; create *empathy* in those who have never experienced mental health challenges; provide *education* on how to support a loved one; and most of all, to provide a sense of *hope* and *belief* for those living with mental health problems that recovery, whatever that may mean for the individual, is possible. But to provide that sense of hope and belief, I first need to share a brief story of where I've been.

In **Part 1**, I will share with you my experience of living with mental health problems. Although my story relates to experiences with post-traumatic stress disorder and major depressive disorder, it has commonality with those experiencing other mental health problems as well. For some of you, my story may resonate with your own experiences and help you to feel less alone. For those supporting and caring for loved ones struggling with their mental health, reading this may help you understand. For some, this may be hard reading, particularly the topic of suicide, so please take care in doing so. But if you feel it is too much, you can skip through to Part 2 for a positive story of hope.

In **Part 2**, I will share my recovery journey, retold in parts from my first book but now including the critical importance of having a recovery *game plan*, and the elements that support recovery. I will introduce my key recovery strategies, how I used them and how they worked for me.

In **Part 3**, I will seek to demonstrate that not only is mental health recovery possible but so too is coming out the other side more resilient than before. I will share my experience of turning life's adversities and challenges into *opportunity* and facing them with a positive mindset of being in control rather than falling into a negative victim mindset. Last of all, I will share how the practice of writing or journaling has helped me process my life events and challenges and how it helps to heal.

One last word on the content of this book. As most of what I have written is based on my *own* experiences, that doesn't mean those experiences, or my beliefs and opinions, are shared by everyone. As I'll say again later, we are all different. We all have different challenges, personalities, abilities and opportunities. But that said, for those struggling to find a way through, I hope what I have shared in this book might provide a spark of belief, even if it's only a little one.

Because even a little spark can light a beacon.

PART 1

MENTAL HEALTH

CHAPTER 1

Depression

In 2012, at the age of forty-two, I experienced the debilitation of major depressive disorder for the first time. It floored me, and I had no answer to it for three long years.

At times I have found it difficult to accurately describe in words what depression looks and feels like. I mean, we all go through periods where we experience depressed moods, but having severe, diagnosable clinical depression is another level altogether. However, I often use the ocean as a metaphor.

I love the ocean and have spent much of my life surfing its swells. For most of my life, even while struggling with PTSD, I rode my board reasonably high on the peaks of those swells and had some moments of pure joy and happiness at the very top. But between the swells of ocean waves are troughs. Occasionally, I faced challenges in life that knocked me off my board into the trough behind. On these occasions, time after time, I drew upon the strategies and resilience I had built throughout my life to climb back onto my board and paddle up onto the next swell, and I knew through life experience that if I kept paddling, I'd *get there*.

In 2012, though, I fell off my metaphorical board, and all the strategies that served me in the past failed to work. Burnout from chronic stress, poor sleep hygiene and alcohol abuse had weakened my resilience. This time, I got stuck in the trough.

For me, the depression experience was like having all light, hope and self-belief extinguished. I had no energy. I stopped boxing and gym training. I stopped surfing. I stopped everything that I previously enjoyed because I no longer experienced enjoyment. I grew a beard and became reclusive. Some days I'd try reading a book and would have to read the same page over and over again because it just didn't sink in. My concentration was so shot up that I'd do things like crossing the road without looking. I lost my sex drive and function, which then fed into my already low self-esteem and sense of worth. I was constantly tired, like a deep, chronic fatigue. Some days I would force myself out of bed to make my kids' lunches for school, and the simple decisions involved in carrying out that task would overwhelm me. Then I would go back to bed, and that's where they'd find me when they came home from school. I was physically and mentally paralysed.

Quite often I would just run out of the house so that

my family wouldn't see me crying. One night I lost it completely, jumped in my car, drove to the headland, stumbled down the grass slope and considered ending it all. I thought about jumping into the boiling ocean from the rock face and, if I survived the fall, swimming so far out that I would never make it back. The very thought of harming myself made me deeply ashamed. I laid down on a wooden bench seat for hours, shivering in the cold ocean wind, crying my eyes out.

For a bloke who had thought himself invincible, full of life and confident beyond description, this sudden capitulation was particularly hard-hitting. The deep depression I had fallen into so suddenly was something I could never have previously imagined. It felt much like grief. It was like the emotional pain of losing someone important in your life but with the absence of two significant factors.

First, when we lose someone, we know the reason for our pain. It is tangible. My depressed mood, at that time, was missing tangible reason. I could not accept my inability to simply pick myself up and snap out of it. *Second*, when we lose someone, we know through the experience of our own lives and others' that life will go on, and at some point, the pain will subside. Every day will be a little better than the one before. But with depression, for a long time, the next day felt worse than the one before. The inner strength that carried me through the challenges of my life, the strength that I had drawn upon to pick myself up when I was down or when facing danger, it was all gone. My defences had collapsed.

I felt weak, and for the first time in my adult life, I felt vulnerable.

▪▪▪

Before depression, I had been a high-achieving, assertive, confident and outgoing detective sergeant in one of the largest police forces in the English-speaking world. My career spanned a quarter of a century across much of the state of New South Wales, including inner-city Sydney, the outback, and large inland and coastal regional towns.

Seven years into my career I married, and over the next twenty years Wendy and I raised three sons, Hugh, Owen and Niam. Our marriage was strong in the beginning but deteriorated in later years for several reasons, for which we both share some responsibility, but my job and the way I handled it was a major contributor. Despite our problems, we raised our sons in a seaside town on the New South Wales north coast, our lifestyle was idyllic, and we had plenty of good times.

During my career I investigated many hundreds of serious crimes, including homicides, drug and organised crime, rapes, child abuse, arson, armed robberies, fatal car accidents and much, much more. I also investigated many dozens of suicides. I was exposed to so much violence and trauma over the years that I can recall only the most personally significant events. For much of my career I thought I could handle everything my job threw at me, and at the worst crime scenes I just put my head down and got on with the job. I was big and strong. I thought myself fearless, formidable and almost bulletproof.

However, in 2012, after completing one of my most high-risk and challenging investigations into an outlaw motorcycle gang, it all came to an end. I experienced what I described then as a devastating mental breakdown, which nine months later ended the career I loved so much, contributed to the ruin of my marriage, and eventually resulted in an attempt to take my own life.

Prior to my breakdown, I had been living with post-traumatic stress disorder (PTSD) in secret for more than eight years. The first clear warning signs began with the onset of distressing nightmares soon after exposure to a horrific homicide, which occurred around the same time I was targeted by an outlaw motorcycle gang in a violent off-duty attack. Every night I would wake from the same nightmare at the point where I was about to be murdered. It was terrifying, and I rarely got back to sleep. I knew it was my work that was causing the nightmares, but back then we had no education about mental health and limited support services. I clearly remember lying in bed one morning and thinking: *What am I going to do about this?* My resolution? I decided to keep it all locked up as a tightly held secret and to tell no one.

Less than fifty percent of people with a diagnosable mental illness seek professional help. For years I was one of the majority of people who don't. There are many common barriers that delay seeking professional help, but there were two in particular that influenced my decision. The first was my own ego.

Over the years I had built a reputation with my colleagues of being tough, and I didn't want to lose that reputation. I didn't want my workmates to think I wasn't strong enough to handle the job. The workplace culture I had grown into was one where we were expected to be tough enough to take anything, and I felt that if anyone knew about my nightmares then I would have failed. The second and probably most significant barrier was that I was terrified of losing my job. Very few of my workmates who declared mental health problems returned to work, and most were medically retired. This created a distorted view that if I was diagnosed with PTSD, my career would be over. What I didn't factor in was that many of them, like me, hadn't sought early intervention and ended up so unwell they could no longer continue.

When I made my decision that morning to keep it secret, I thought to myself: *No one dies of a nightmare – just put up with them, suck it up and don't ever tell anyone.* And that's what I did for more than eight years. But unfortunately for me, because of a complete lack of education and training, I did not recognise the many other signs, symptoms and behaviours of PTSD that I was exhibiting. And when those signs, symptoms and behaviours began to hijack my life and cause absolute chaos, particularly at home, I failed to join the dots and make the connection with a significant mental health problem. In fact, it wasn't until I received treatment many years later that everything finally made sense.

CHAPTER 2

Post-traumatic stress disorder

Trauma-related mental health problems are often complicated, but they are also common. There are many life experiences and risk factors that may lead an individual to develop such problems, so we should never judge or compare with others.

In other words, I experienced many traumatic events in my life, both during and after my police career, but I never judge what others are going through by comparing their experiences to mine. Regardless of the causes, what was most relevant was the impact PTSD had on my life and the lives of those closest to me. I'll start with *hypervigilance*.

I could rarely relax. I was constantly alert for danger and scanning for threats, particularly in public places like shopping centres, and in cafés and restaurants I never sat with my back to the door. I describe my threat-level bar graph as being green for relaxed and red for combat-ready. For many years I lived permanently in the yellow to orange region, so it didn't take much to flip me over to red. At night, if I heard even the slightest noise in my house I would flip straight to red, get out of bed and patrol through the house to make sure my family were safe. My sympathetic nervous system (fight, flight, freeze) had largely taken over. Combined with the nightmares, hypervigilance contributed to the next problem, *chronically poor sleep.*

From the onset of my nightmares, I experienced serious problems with sleep. I'd often get off to sleep okay, but most nights I would wake a couple of hours later and fail to get back to sleep. Once awake, my brain would switch on and I'd lie in bed ruminating over work and other stressors. Sleep problems are a very common symptom of many mental health conditions, including anxiety and depression. There are so many physical and psychological restorative functions that occur during healthy sleep, the benefits of which I was denied due to chronically poor sleep. For many years I survived on between two and five hours of sleep a night, and that is simply not sustainable. Living on very little sleep also contributed to other problems, including *anger* and *irritability.*

Being constantly tired, stressed and wound up with raw nerves led to me developing a hair-trigger temper, where sudden loud noises, like someone dropping crockery in the kitchen, would set me off. At work I became increasingly aggressive when dealing with confrontational situations, not only out on the street but also internally with difficult colleagues and managers. At home I was often in an irritable mood and not the easiest person to get along with. I'd frequently come home from work and need to be left alone until I could decompress. Regular irritability and bad moods put a strain on relationships with my wife and kids, as did another problem: *emotional numbing.*

This psychological symptom of PTSD had a destructive impact on my personal life, particularly my relationships. I don't know the science of why emotional numbing is such a common symptom of trauma; I'll leave that to the experts. But as for my own experience, I think the best way to describe it is this: whenever I witnessed something horrific, dealt with raw grief and loss or nursed victims of crime through sometimes years of court cases, I either avoided or suppressed all the normal human emotions that I should have experienced so I could get on with the job. The more I did it, the less I was able to tap into my emotions, even at times when I should have. It was a protective mechanism to avoid hurt and distress, and over time I largely lost the ability to experience positive feelings like happiness and love. At home I was often withdrawn and experienced feelings of disconnection, mostly towards those closest to me.

So for those eight years, there was a lot going

on. Lots of destructive emotional and behavioural problems had a significant negative impact on my life and the lives of those around me. As I've mentioned, I had made a choice to keep the nightmares secret, but when it came to the other problems I have described above, I didn't make a connection. I remember there were so many times when I lay awake at night plagued with thoughts I believed no one else would think, usually involving violence. I clearly remember driving to work one morning and a red traffic light not only caused me to stop my car but also snapped me out of a violent 'what if' scenario that was playing out in my head. I sat there watching pedestrians crossing the road and green light traffic moving off, all the while thinking that I was going crazy. *Who else would think the sort of things you think about?*

On two separate occasions, years apart, I challenged my decision to keep my problems secret and took the terrifying step of seeking help confidentially through counselling. It wasn't what I would describe as meaningful help, though, more like dipping my toe in the water, and both times I didn't feel comfortable enough to open up in an honest way. So instead of committing to meaningful help, I did what is also very common with people living with undiagnosed mental illness: I relied on my own coping strategies.

The only positive coping strategy I relied on during those last eight years of my career was exercise, the benefits of which I'll discuss later. Most of my coping strategies, however, were negative and maladaptive, perhaps helping me survive in the short to medium term, but in the long term compounding the fallout of my deteriorating mental health. The first one I will discuss is *avoidance*.

When I made my decision to keep the nightmares secret, I also considered that, in order to protect myself from further damage, I should avoid exposure to traumatic experiences as much as possible. That sounds all well in theory, but with a job where not only looking at traumatic crime scenes but deeply *analysing* them was a necessity, accomplishing that avoidance was difficult. I tried limiting my trauma exposure to the crime scenes and photographs that I absolutely needed to see and avoided all else. I also increasingly found myself avoiding crime novels and violent movies with an incorrect assumption that these too could do further damage. Another form of avoidance to help me cope was *substance abuse*.

The police force I joined had a substantial drinking culture – little wonder given the complete lack of support services in those days – and from a young age I had fallen in with that culture. My use of alcohol back then was mostly social, for having a good time. In later years, though, alcohol served to numb me out and provide some escape. When using alcohol, I had the feeling it helped calm me down, but looking back now with the benefit of hindsight, alcohol was making my mental health problems worse. Alcohol may have had a calming effect in the moment, but when I was coming down from it, the anxiety associated with PTSD became more severe, particularly at night, worsening my already poor sleeping habits. It was a vicious cycle. I describe alcohol as a *mood amplifier*: if I was in a good, social mood it made me more so, but if I was feeling down or angry about something, it made me more irritable and depressed. Alcohol abuse was a significant contributor to my relationship problems, especially those in my marriage, which was also suffering under my next coping strategy: *self-destructive risk-taking behaviours.*

There was a direct correlation between the onset and worsening of PTSD, and increased reckless behaviour. Nightmares, problems with sleep, fears of going crazy, being a target of violent crime and a disintegrating marriage left me feeling vulnerable and, I guess, unsafe. To counter these vulnerabilities, I sought ways to make myself feel tougher and more invincible. I increased the frequency of my gym sessions and took up boxing with the intent of getting fit, but also of becoming more formidable. At work I was taking lots of unnecessary risks, always looking for opportunities to place myself in harm's way, and on occasions I injured myself in the process. All of this fed my ego, which started to get a little out of control, and as a result I wasn't the nicest person to live with.

I hold a belief that mental health problems can influence poor behaviour, but that doesn't mean they always provide an excuse. I have always owned my actions and never blamed them on my mental health problems, especially when it comes to the way I have treated others. There was, however, an equivalence between my deteriorating mental health and my deteriorating marriage. And at those times when I felt my marriage was doomed to failure and I lost all hope, I recklessly spiralled into marital self-destruct, including infidelity and late-night social drinking, with little care for the consequences or the hurt I would cause (I'll come back to this later). By this time, I barely knew who I was. I felt like I just had to keep running harder and harder to stay ahead of the things I was dealing with that I didn't understand, which leads into my last coping strategy: *my job.*

It's a little ironic that in trying to escape my undiagnosed mental health problems, I turned to the thing that had caused them: my work. Burying myself in my job helped me survive on multiple levels. My colleagues and I shared a common bond and camaraderie built on shared experiences and, at times, danger, so the only people who I felt truly understood me and accepted me for who I was were my workmates. At work was where I was most comfortable and felt most connected, and socialising with my colleagues after work, often at the expense of my family, was an extension of that feeling. But aside from social connection, my work also provided an escape through stimulation and distraction.

I was the leader of a proactive unit responsible for the investigation of serious drug and property crime, including armed robberies. This involved the regular execution of search warrants, performing surveillance and other stressful, high-risk work that fed me loads of adrenaline. I would often arrive at work feeling tired and worn down from poor sleep, but those feelings would be short-lived once I plugged into the adrenaline socket of my work. It wasn't just the physically risky nature of my work that gave me a buzz either – I was also stimulated by the stress of my work and the challenges I set myself. I was always looking for the next big job, and when I found one, I'd bury myself in it, sometimes for many months, until reaching a successful conclusion. Then I'd start looking for another, and the next needed to be bigger than the last, and this cycle went on and on. It was like some sort of manic defence to keeping me running and out of reach of the claws of the PTSD that had been trying to bring me down for many years. There is some tie-in here with *avoidance* and *risk-taking*, I guess, and like all my other coping strategies, single-minded focus on work had a negative impact on my family life.

Riding high on the excitement and stress of my work helped me survive for many years, but eventually, the old rule that 'what goes up must come down' was very true for me.

CHAPTER 3

Stress and burnout

Considering the high levels of stress I was under for the duration of my law enforcement career, it would have been helpful to understand how stress was affecting me so I could work on managing it a little better. I have a good understanding now, and here's how I describe it.

Our stress response has evolved primarily to increase our chances of surviving life-threatening or other challenging situations, like being attacked by a predator. In my police experience, whenever I faced a dangerous situation, my brain sent messages that triggered a fight, flight or freeze response, causing a rapid change in my physical, emotional and psychological function. Stress hormones including adrenaline and cortisol were pumped into my bloodstream to supercharge my mind and body. My airways opened up and my breathing became faster to take in more oxygen. Oxygen-rich blood was diverted from areas of my body that were not needed for fight or escape, like the digestive system, to areas where it was most needed, like the brain, heart and muscles. Sensory functions like sight, hearing, touch, taste and smell became sharper and more acute. This stress response (the sympathetic nervous system) continued until such time that I registered the threat had passed. This is exactly what my stress response was designed for: short bursts for a few minutes to help me survive danger. Even a short burst of this acute stress used up so much of my physical and mental resources that I often felt exhausted afterwards.

The problem, though, was that I was experiencing this acute stress response far too regularly, mostly for non-life-threatening situations, like the hypervigilance experiences I have already described or the ongoing pressure of high-risk, challenging work. I was spending too much time wound up in a fight-or-flight state of arousal and flooded with stress hormones at times when I should have been in a state of 'rest and digest' (the parasympathetic nervous system). I knew stress was contributing to my poor sleep hygiene, but what I didn't know was the damage this stress was doing to my physical and mental health. Physically, prolonged periods of high stress were compromising my immune system, resulting in skin problems and leaving me susceptible to infection. Although there was nothing wrong with my heart, I often experienced chest pains and heart palpitations, common symptoms of stress and anxiety.

I wouldn't say I was addicted to the stimulation of stress – more accurately, I was probably *dependent* on it to help me cope and escape. I was constantly running at maximum stress capacity for many years, which the stress response is not designed for, and like a car engine that is stuck in high revs, eventually something was going to break.

Twice during my career I had pushed myself right up to the cliff edge of burnout, the first around the twelve-year mark and the second about five years later. Both occurred during long periods of almost impossible work demands where I felt completely overwhelmed and unable to see a way through. I was always exhausted and emotionally drained, and I became even more irritable, with increasingly negative attitudes and cynicism towards my job and life in general. On both occasions, the most obvious signs I was at breaking point were when I lost all motivation, dreaded going to work and completely lost any sense of the enjoyment and pleasure that my career had aways provided me. It was when I reached this point that my self-awareness would finally kick in and, thankfully, on both occasions I took proactive steps to back away from the cliff. I organised time away from my normal work as a detective and went back to uniform for a few months. I dedicated time to my family and friends and got back to doing more of the things that I enjoyed, mainly surfing and fishing. I was refilling my emotional bucket, and because of that, on both occasions I was able to return to my role as a detective with renewed enthusiasm, motivation and enjoyment. However, on the third occasion that I reached the cliff edge, I took one step too far.

▪ ▪ ▪

For the previous eighteen months I had been leading the most challenging investigation into an outlaw motorcycle gang of my entire career. During the final nine months of that job, I barely had a day off. I was on my phone constantly, buried neck-deep in danger, professional risk and incredible work demands. At home my marriage was falling apart, which added another level of stress and worry. I was running at my maximum stress capacity 24/7 with very little sleep, pushing myself to the absolute outer limits of survival. And right about then, my father-in-law died.

As a young eighteen-year-old recruit at the New South Wales Police Force Academy, I was put through specialised driver training, and one day a veteran driving instructor shared some advice I have never forgotten. He told us to *never* drive at our maximum driving ability in a high-speed chase, because if we did and something unexpected happened, we would have nothing left with which to navigate it. He advised us to never drive at more than eight-tenths of our maximum ability, so if that something unexpected happened, we would have another two-tenths up our sleeve to navigate it. I have often thought about that advice when reflecting on my journey towards eventual burnout. I had been running at my maximum stress capacity for a very long time, and when my wife's father died, with the associated mountain of grief in our family, I had nothing left to navigate it. I didn't back away from the cliff edge – I ran off it.

After a week of extensive travel with my wife and kids, planning and attending the funeral and dealing with the related death-in-the-family processes, I went back to work. This time, though, I lacked that which was needed most: enthusiasm. The team I had under me were still firing on all cylinders and keen to keep pushing ahead with the job. I, on the other hand, suddenly found myself wanting to wind it all up and get it finished. This was extremely out of character for me, but I just felt so exhausted that I didn't think I could push on any further. My team was right, though: we did have more work to do before the arrest phase, and so I pushed on.

Two months later I found myself standing at a lectern looking out over the faces of dozens of colleagues I was about to send into harm's way to bring our investigation to a successful conclusion. Normally when delivering a briefing before a big job, I would be fired up and full of inspiration, but this time I found myself feeling flat and sad. I didn't know why, and no one else would have noticed because by now

I had become a master at masking my mental health problems. By the end of that day, we had concluded one of the most complex and successful organised crime investigations ever run in regional New South Wales. Professionally, it was my highest ever achievement. I was at the top of my game. I had promotions to look forward to and a long career left in front of me. My mood that day, like my career, should have been soaring. I should have been feeling euphoric, like I always did after a big win, but instead, I felt very few positive feelings at all.

Over the next few weeks, my mood plummeted hard and fast, and there was nothing I could do to stop it. All the coping strategies I had relied on for so long to keep me going, all the alcohol and adrenaline, not only ceased to work but were making me worse. My already poor sleeping habits deteriorated to the point where some nights I didn't sleep at all. I went to work every day, pushing on with mop-up operations from our job, but even the effort required to fake it, to put on a front that there was nothing wrong, took so much of my remaining energy that I barely had anything left. At home I seesawed between deeply anxious and deeply depressed. I was extremely irritable, overreacting to everything that annoyed me, real or perceived. I battled on for four or five weeks until eventually my tank was empty. I had nothing left. I had never in my life felt so *lifeless.*

Finally accepting that I was in bad shape and

unable to cope on my own, I looked up the website of a world leader in mental health research, the Black Dog Institute (BDI) in Australia. I found there a very helpful self-screening tool, and because it was completely confidential, I decided to give it a go.

I was asked questions about my mood and feelings over the past couple of weeks, and for each question I clicked on the answer most applicable to me. The process took about ten minutes, and at the end of it I was provided with an assessment report. My results indicated that it was likely I was experiencing depression, anxiety and post-traumatic stress. Rather than being shocked, I felt somewhat relieved. Now I had a medical name for everything I had experienced for many years, and it wasn't all in my head. These results also convinced me that I needed to make a full commitment to seeking out professional help, so I set about doing exactly that.

CHAPTER 4

Impact on family

Over the next five years of treatment and recovery, I attended more than two hundred sessions with doctors, psychologists and psychiatrists. One of the many things I have learned from that extensive experience is that good, effective professional therapy is reliant on *trust* and *rapport*, both of which often take time to build.

As mentioned, I twice took cautious steps towards getting professional help in earlier years. These attempts were unsuccessful for several reasons, including my fear of the consequences if I made full disclosures, but mainly because I just didn't feel any connection with the clinicians I saw. I had been tentative in how much I disclosed while I tested the water, but each time I wasn't confident that they *got* me, which I used as an excuse to stop going. A better choice would have been to ask for referrals to see others until I found someone who was the right fit for me. Eventually that happened, in no small part owing to the knowledge, experience and care of my GP.

For most people living in Australia, visiting a general practitioner is a good initial step in seeking treatment for mental health problems. The first benefit of visiting a GP is the significant crossover between mental and physical health, both of which doctors are trained to assess and manage. The second benefit is that once a GP has made an assessment, they can put together mental health care plans that can be subsidised by Medicare, and then under that plan the patient can be referred to other specialist clinicians such as psychologists and psychiatrists for treatment.

I clearly remember the day I arrived for my first mental health assessment with my family GP, Dr John Kramer. I sat in front of him with tears streaming down my face, so overwhelmed with despair that I could barely speak, and even if I could I probably wouldn't have known where to start. What John did for me from that day I consider a blueprint of how a GP should care for patients with mental health problems. He didn't rush. He displayed genuine empathy and care. He made a plan, and as part of that plan he considered clinicians to whom he would shortly refer me. He had a list of clinicians in our local area, and he made sure he chose a psychologist and psychiatrist who he knew would likely be the right fit for me.

For the next five years, Dr Kramer, Annette (my

psychologist) and Peter (my psychiatrist) became my team. As a psychologist, Annette's position in the team was primarily to lead me through talking therapy but also some exposure therapy and mindfulness/meditation practice. As my psychiatrist, Peter's position was primarily to prescribe and manage medications, but he also led me through some therapies I'll talk about later. And pulling all of this into a well-organised, co-ordinated process was my GP, Dr Kramer. As my psychological conditions were accepted as a work injury, John wasn't just my doctor – he was also my *advocate* in supporting me through a sometimes challenging WorkCover process.

In the beginning I was so unwell that I had appointments with my psychologist and psychiatrist every week. Peter diagnosed me with post-traumatic stress disorder and major depressive disorder, for which he prescribed antipsychotic and antidepressant medications, but my mental health problems had become so deeply embedded over the years that any hope of a short recovery then back to work was unrealistic. A collective decision was reached between my clinicians, the clinicians engaged by my employer and, to some extent, me that the career that I had loved so much for my entire adult life was over.

With that decision made, I was medically retired on 28 March 2013. What lay ahead of me was a five-year journey to hell and back that would take me to the lowest point my life could possibly reach but also provide me with a sense of meaning and purpose I otherwise could never have imagined.

▪ ▪ ▪

The three years following my retirement were like living on a horrible rollercoaster. From high anxiety with PTSD I'd crash and burn into long periods of severely depressed moods. I was not in any way ready for the pure, raw grief that hit me from the loss of my career. I expected leaving the police force to solve all my mental health problems, but all it did, at least in the first year or so, was add another one – grief.

It was hard to reconcile the grief because the associated loss had so many layers. Loss of my career. Loss of a dream. Loss of purpose. Loss of self-esteem. Loss of meaning. And loss of *identity.* For my entire adult life since the age of nineteen, I had been a police officer. For twenty-five years, everybody knew me as Detective Craig Semple. It was a job that provided me with prestige. It was a job that was dangerous and exciting. It was a job that gave me purpose. It was a job in which I really made a difference. But when all of that disappeared, the loss was sudden, unplanned and crippling, and it complicated my battle with depression. It was just so hard to let go.

One morning after the kids left for school, I drove down to a local beachside café, bought a coffee and parked down at the boat ramp to watch the ocean. At least that was my intent. Instead I found myself watching two cars parked next to each other, the activity of the occupants leaving me in no doubt it was a drug deal. I was fixated, even calling my old workmates to get them onto it. I knew I had to stop, to switch off, but it was so hard. I had been mentally and physically hardwired over two decades to scan for threat, suspicious behaviour, suspicious people, always looking for badness. It wasn't something that could be turned off like a switch because it was a deeply embedded instinct. It was an asset as a detective, but now it just made me feel like I had gone completely crazy. My entire life felt like one enormous trigger, which sometimes even led to confrontations I should have avoided. Then I'd have to deal with the aftermath, the feelings of stupidity and shame that would send me back into deeply depressed moods. It was a tough way to live, not just on me but also my family.

I remember one afternoon my three teenage sons arrived home from school and I noticed the eldest, seventeen-year-old Hugh, looked troubled. Thinking something bad had happened at school, I said, 'Mate, what's wrong? You don't look very happy.'

Avoiding eye contact, he replied, 'I'm right, Dad. It's nothing.'

I walked around the counter, sat on a stool next to him and said, 'I know something is wrong, mate, I can see it. What's up?'

Then he just let it out. 'I'm so scared that I will never see you happy again!'

And with that, Hughie burst into tears. I wrapped him in my arms and hugged him tight while he cried and cried. And then I cried too. I cried because in my arms I held the true impact of my battle with depression and PTSD. I could feel Hughie's pain, and from that I knew his brothers would be similarly affected. I felt responsible. I felt *guilty*, like this was all my fault, though I was plagued with guilt for plenty of other reasons as well.

Regardless of how unwell I was during the last years of my career, I still had choices, and during the early months of my psychological treatment I reflected deeply on those choices. The fact that I had very little emotional connection or support in my marriage was no excuse to look for that connection and support elsewhere, but I did, and I shouldn't have. My sudden psychological breakdown was like being woken up from a bad dream. It was like all the armour I had built around myself fell away, and although I was severely unwell, I was *me* again. So when I looked back at who I had become, what I had done to my marriage and the hurt I had caused, I didn't like what I saw, then regret and guilt settled in on top of everything else. And as much as remorse is a good motivator for behavioural change, feelings of regret and guilt are food for depression. They *feed* it.

■■■

For three years I attended hundreds of hours of therapy sessions with my clinicians and others, including a three-month program at a traumatic stress clinic. I was introduced to lots of treatments I found helpful, including yoga and mindfulness/meditation, but also others I found less effective. Some treatments, like cognitive behaviour therapy (CBT), for example, had no chance of being effective because I simply lacked belief in them, so I didn't commit. This lack of belief not only in some of my treatments but, more importantly, in *myself* left me feeling like I was treading water wearing lead boots and in a constant struggle to keep my head above the surface.

And at the times when I felt like I was losing that struggle, when I lost hope and felt like I was drowning, I often considered taking my own life.

CHAPTER 5

Shining a light on suicide

Many people consider the topic of suicide dark, depressing and difficult to talk about. It's a topic that is largely pushed into the shadows where no one can see it, so I'm going to shine a little light on it here.

As a police detective, one of my core duties was to investigate suicides. Over a twenty-five-year career I investigated dozens of suicide deaths, mostly men who had been battling depression. I could never understand it. Arriving to witness the aftermath, the devastation of family and friends, I just couldn't comprehend someone reaching a point where life was so bad that killing themselves was an option. With no education about mental health, I was quite ignorant, caring for those left behind but lacking empathy for the person whose life was lost. These days, with the benefit of insight gained through my own battle with depression and suicide, I have a much deeper understanding.

During my darkest periods of depression, suicidal thoughts were a regular companion. They terrified me. I was so scared that I might one day become one of those whose deaths I had investigated. What is important to note is that I did *not* want to die – I just wanted the endless emotional pain to stop. Curiously, it wasn't the knowledge of what I would put my family through that kept me from suicide but the thought of the trauma for my old workmates when they were called to investigate. What I was going through was so incredibly painful that I could not allow myself to pass it on to anyone else, which was a good deterrent to acting on my thoughts but also made me feel trapped.

I was never completely honest with my clinicians about thoughts of suicide. I had a misguided fear that if I told them, I would find myself admitted to a hospital, and I didn't want that to happen. Maybe if I had known more about it, especially how incredibly common it is for people to experience suicidal ideation, I may have been more open and honest, but back then I felt deeply ashamed and too embarrassed to say anything.

If I had been honest, my clinicians would have been able to work with me on measures to keep me safe when a suicide crisis took hold. One of those measures could have been educating my family and those closest to me about the warning signs and what to do if they recognised them. But as it was, everyone was blind to the danger I was in. Everyone but me.

The difficult reality with recovery from mental

illness is that for most of us, life doesn't take a pause. I still had to face other challenges in life, including the grief associated with the loss of my career, marital crisis, financial pressures and more, all of which complicated my forward progress. Life rarely offers a ceasefire, and it certainly didn't for me. I was being hit with one adversity after another. The worst crisis of my life, involving my discovery of unforgivable behaviour by my father, occurred about fifteen months into my medical retirement, and it would have been a challenge even if I was in the best of health. Most of what happened back then I cannot share for the privacy and protection of my family, but I clearly remember making the phone call reporting my father to the police, my old colleagues. I remember the heartbreak, the shame and the anger.

For those entire three years since retirement, it had been impossible to get my head into some clean, fresh air. And then came the final straw when my wife asked for a separation. Until then I had resisted acting on my suicidal thoughts, but on the afternoon of 13 March 2015, soon after my separation, I felt so worn down and utterly depressed that it was like some switch flicked off and my resistance vanished.

I made a plan. Having made a plan, I experienced a sad sense of relief. The time between making that plan and acting on it was about one hour. Shortly after carrying out my plan, I realised I had made a terrible, terrible mistake and called upon my eldest son, Hugh, to help me. About half an hour later I found myself in a hospital emergency bed hooked up to monitors. I was terrified. I realised I didn't want to die, I wanted to live, and I had to wait four anxious hours before I knew for sure that I would. During that time I made a solemn promise, to my son and to myself, that this would never happen again and that I would find a way to get back on my feet and reclaim my life. I was lucky: I got a second chance where many don't. The most important lesson I learned from the whole experience is this:

If you are feeling suicidal, please tell someone. Ask them to assist you to get professional help and to keep you safe. Call a crisis line. Please don't keep it a secret. In the moment you may not feel like there is any point in living, but if you give it time, the worst of those feelings will pass as they did for me.

It is unfortunate that I had to give myself and my family such a terrible fright to realise that suicide was not the best option to deal with my problems, but that's what happened and there is nothing I can do to change it. But I did make good on the promise I made that night, and I did reclaim my life. It didn't happen overnight, and it took a lot of hard work, but it was so worth it.

This is how it happened.

LIFELINE: 13 11 14

PART 2

RECOVERY

CHAPTER 6

Game-planning recovery

I woke around 8 a.m., opened my eyes and stared at the ceiling as the events of the night before started to filter into my consciousness.

I remembered my panic the moment I realised I had made a grave mistake. I remembered Hughie, at eighteen years of age, having to drive me to the hospital and then sit by the bed holding my hand while he watched the numbers on the monitors. I remembered my declaration to him, and to myself, that I would never do anything like that again. I remembered the intensity of the fear of death I experienced, a fear that proved to me beyond doubt that I had something left in me. That my time was not up. That I still wanted to live.

I knew I had to get up and face the world. Face my family. Face myself. I got out of bed, a bed I no longer shared, and padded into the bathroom. The floor was still littered with upturned drawers, empty blister packs and toiletries. I tidied it all up and stood, shirtless, to face myself in the mirror. Hospital electrode patches were still stuck on my chest and I took a real good look at them, so I would never forget, before I slowly peeled them off my body. I had a warm, comforting shower, dressed, walked from my bedroom to the kitchen to make a cup of tea, then sat down in the lounge room.

I started to think about how I was going to explain all this to my family, to everyone. Eventually I realised there was nothing I could say that would accurately convey the depth of what had occurred. Of how it had become so bad that I could even contemplate the decision I made the night before. So I picked up my laptop, opened a blank document, and started typing. At the time, it seemed the only way I could explain it.

The Door

It is a door. It is in the back room of my mind. It doesn't sell itself to me. It doesn't open and wave me through. It doesn't need to because it has a unique, tempting appeal.

I only confront it when I leave the front room, the room where I feel content, safe. From there I drift down a hall. Sometimes the journey down this hall is short. Sometimes it's long. At the end of the hall is the back room. The back room has two doors, one to the left and one to the right.

The left door is the one I usually take. It's the one that takes me the long way back to the front room. It is a hard journey that requires lots of effort. Every time I have taken the left door, I have made it back to the front room where I am safe again.

The door to the right is different. It is different from the left door for one reason. It doesn't lead back to the front room. It requires little effort. It offers sure relief from pain and grief. Every time I have entered the back room, I have seen the right-side door.

I am always scared of it because I know what it offers. I don't want to be tempted. I don't want to open it. If I go through it the door will close behind me and never open again. I will be lost forever.

But now I have opened the right-side door. I walked through it. And it didn't close behind me. It stayed open and I found my way back. I had a second chance.

The right-side door no longer exists in the back room of my mind. I turned my back on it and it has gone. I should never have entered that door.

I am so lucky.

▪▪▪

That afternoon the mental health crisis team arrived at my house to make sure I was safe, and there was no shadow of doubt when I assured them that I was. I'd given myself a huge fright. It was a real wake-up call, and I declared to myself that it would *never* happen again. I wanted to live and live well. I felt it. It was real.

But a simple positive affirmation wasn't going to fix things. To fix things, I needed to get well. I couldn't rely on others to fix things for me. It was my responsibility. Not my doctor's or my family's or the insurance company's – the responsibility was *mine.* I needed to find a way to turn things around. I was in a state of calm, and for the first time in a long while I had clarity of thought. For the next few days, I sat in my lounge room with a notepad and pen and quietly reflected on my situation and the events that had led me there. I wrote it all down, everything, so I could make sense of it all.

One of the first things I identified was that before I could move forward, I needed to find forgiveness for myself. I couldn't change my past; I couldn't change the mistakes I had made in my marriage or the hurt I had caused. I had to let go of the regret and guilt that had weighed me down for so long – I had punished myself enough. When I weighed up all the good I had done in my life with the not so good, the balance was well in favour of the good. So I decided to draw a line in the sand, accept my mistakes, commit to never making them again and forgive myself fully. Self-forgiveness allowed me to start looking forward rather than back. Then I moved to the next issue: my father.

I couldn't change history. My father did what he did and there was nothing I could do to change that. I couldn't alter the fact that throughout my life my dad had not been a good role model, so I needed to let go of the shame and anger and move on. I thought long and hard on it, and in the end I decided to make two promises to myself. The first was to never follow in my dad's footsteps, which meant I would never betray and intentionally, or even carelessly, hurt anybody ever again. The second promise was that I would use the negative experience of my relationship with my father to forever motivate me to be the best dad I could be to my three boys. That might not make me the world's best dad, but I would always be better than the one I had. And when the time came, my challenge to my three boys would be to try to be a better dad than the one they had. And if they chose to, they could pass the same challenge to their sons, and that way we will all keep trying. I made peace with that.

I then moved on to the next issue. I realised that something I had given up way back at the beginning of my retirement was *control*. On retirement from the police force I had fallen into the workers compensation system. I had a reliance on insurance companies for financial support and my clinicians for medical support. That dependency, and the need to constantly provide evidence of illness and injury, served to reinforce a negative victim mindset that others had control of my life, not me. I needed to find a way to reclaim that control and set my own direction. To do that, I needed to make a *plan*.

I think my professional experience may have helped. Whenever I was faced with a serious crime to investigate, I came up with a strategic investigation plan. Whenever I had a search warrant to execute,

I prepared a plan. For every professional challenge I faced as a cop, I came up with a plan. During the previous three years I had faced the most significant personal challenges of my life, and not once did I think to sit down and write out a plan. I did now. I decided to prepare a strategic, written game plan for my recovery. The idea fired me up with enthusiasm and, for the first time in three years, a sense of *hope*.

My recovery game plan required strategies, and for those I went hunting. From my bedroom I pulled out all the bags and folders of resources and homework accumulated from over two hundred hours of clinical psychological appointments over the last three years. I took it out to the lounge room, sorted through and wrote down a list of all the strategies I had been taught during those sessions. They included exercise, mindfulness/meditation, writing memoir, cognitive behaviour therapy (CBT), yoga, planning pleasurable activities, and a few others. I took a good look at the list and conceded that for some of the strategies I had not given one hundred percent commitment, and for others I had given none. To some extent, depression robbed me of the required motivation and effort, but for some of the strategies, like CBT, I simply lacked belief. Maintaining motivation and commitment was going to be a significant challenge moving forward, so I knew I needed to set realistic goals and keep my plan achievable not just for when I was at my best but also for when I was at my worst. I made a decision.

I would set a small, achievable action to practise each strategy on my list every day from that day on. Just one for each. My idea was that setting small goals would encourage motivation, minimise the risk of surrender and give me something to build on over time. For each strategy I gave careful thought and customised an action to best fit me, my interests and my abilities. I didn't rush it – in fact, there was one strategy that required a lot of work, so the development of my game plan took a few days. But even the process itself of working on my goal-focused plan gave me a sense of purpose. I will shortly share those strategies, how I used them and how they worked for me, but with the following qualification.

These strategies are all evidence-based and worked for me, but that doesn't mean they will necessarily be the best fit for others. Although I hope to inspire people to give these a go, it is important that individuals on a recovery journey try a variety of strategies and therapies then work with those that are best for them with consideration of their own challenges, abilities, support networks and opportunities. We are all different, and what worked for me may not necessarily work for others, but what I seek to demonstrate is that regardless of the strategies used, what is most important is the *plan*.

▪▪▪

I now had a plan, but before I moved forward with it, I took some time to identify and rectify anything that posed a threat to success.

The first issue was my dependency on medications. I decided to end my reliance on the antidepressants and antipsychotics I had been obediently taking for three long years. The medications had the effect of numbing me, dulling the human experience in addition to many other side effects. My gut instinct was telling me that those medications were not allowing me to properly process and *feel* the things I needed to in order to get well. Although I believed I needed them in the beginning, I could not see the reason in blindly following a process that so far simply hadn't worked. My psychiatrist strongly advised against my decision, but by now I believed I was the best expert on me.

Tapering off medication caused lots of side effects, so following medical advice on how to manage it was important. Gradually, though, I replaced reliance on pills with a commitment to my recovery game plan strategies and behavioural change. I don't ever recommend others do what I did. This was my journey, and I believe sharing what I did is necessary in the interests of transparency, but current research and guidelines for the treatment of PTSD in emergency service workers now contradicts the pharmaceutical therapy I was prescribed.

The second issue was substance use. For many years during my working life, alcohol had been a maladaptive coping strategy I used to help get me through. For the three years after my career ended I was still using alcohol, although I had substantially cut down. I no longer considered myself a problem drinker, but I did acknowledge that *any* alcohol use had the potential to diminish the efficacy of the strategies I was committing to and worsen depression and anxiety, especially considering the decision I made about medications. So to reduce that risk I decided to totally abstain from alcohol until such time that I was well on the road to recovery.

The third issue was my environment. Since my separation a few months earlier I had been living in the same house as my wife, me upstairs and her downstairs. This arrangement had been causing me loads of additional distress and had led to my suicide attempt, but I guess I was sticking it out in the hope she would reconsider. I knew that continuing any longer with this arrangement would just keep dragging me down and pose a serious risk to my recovery, so I made a firm decision. I decided to accept my wife's decision with dignity, move out and find my own place to live. I was mitigating risk by removing myself from a negative environment, taking back control of my life, and giving myself a chance to start over again.

As it turned out, my wife and I reconciled, maybe because for the first time she saw hope in me, or maybe because of some self-reflection, or possibly both, but I was soon invited back home to try again. I'll come back to this later, but at that point in my game plan, for the first time in a long time, I was starting to look forward to something instead of looking back at all that was lost. While for the last three years I had been going around in circles, now I had a sense of direction. For three years I had felt like a victim, but now I felt like I was taking back control. It was time to put my plan into action, and this is how it happened.

CHAPTER 7

Exercise

Before my breakdown, I surfed nearly every day. Each morning before work, if I wasn't boxing, I was surfing. On my days off I surfed. I loved it. Then after my breakdown, I didn't surf much at all. If I did make the effort to put the board in and drive to the beach, more often than not I'd just sit in the car watching the surf, trying to find every reason *not* to go out. I couldn't tap into the pleasure I once received from surfing due to my depressed moods, so I tended to avoid it.

I considered this when I was working on my game plan and my primary action of exercise. I decided that every day, regardless of my mood, I would put the board in my car, drive to the beach and paddle out. All I had to do was get wet. If I only stayed out for a couple of minutes then that was okay – the commitment was just to get out there, and if I did that, I could congratulate myself and head home if I wanted to. One small, achievable action.

Setting a small goal made it easier to maintain motivation, even on the days when my mood was low and I didn't feel like putting in the effort. I'd just say to myself, 'Mate, all you have to do is get down there, jump in and get wet, then you can go back home.' More often than not, once in the water I'd instantly feel much better, so I'd stay out for a surf and benefit from the physical activity. Surfing also created opportunities for social connection, which was an added benefit. For three years I had mostly kept to myself, reclusive at times, but when surfing I'd often get talking to other local surfers. After a few weeks of progress I started adding other exercise activities to my plan, like rejoining yoga classes, going on bush hikes and getting back to weight training at the gym. Exercise helped reduce the frequency and severity of my depressed moods and reduced the intensity of my PTSD-related anxiety and stress. It worked firstly by changing my mood chemistry.

In Chapter 3 I discussed our stress response, the release of stress hormones into the bloodstream, including adrenaline and cortisol, and the adverse impact of excessive stress on our bodies and minds. The severe stress I had experienced for the three years since my police career ended had such an impact on my immune system that my body was shedding toxins through my skin in the form of blisters, mainly on my arms and legs, leading to poorly healed sores, and I had so much stress-related inflammation that it affected my physical health at every level.

Exercise, however, helped my body burn off the adrenaline and cortisol flooding my system, reducing the negative impact of stress on my physical health. The stress blisters stopped appearing and I felt physically better from the reduced inflammation. My mood also improved because as well as burning off all the stress chemistry, exercise served to induce the release of mood-boosting, stress-relieving hormones including endorphins and dopamine. Endorphins are our bodies' natural painkiller. When we experience pain or when our bodies are put under stress through exercise, our pain receptors trigger the release of endorphins into our bloodstream like a narcotic. Not only do they help block pain but endorphins also have a flow-on effect of making us feel happier. So exercise helped in my recovery on a psychological level as well.

Commitment to exercise allowed me to enjoy a positive feeling of achievement every day. It increased motivation for my other game plan actions and goals. It energised me, cleared my head, improved the quality of my sleep, boosted my immune system and improved my overall physical health. I not only started *feeling* better, when I looked in the mirror, I could see I *looked* better, which helped rebuild my self-esteem.

Regular, *enjoyable* exercise became the foundation around which I built my eventual recovery and remains the key foundation for me maintaining that recovery to this day. When encouraging others to consider exercise to better manage mental health or problems with stress, I offer the following tips:

- **Make an exercise plan**. It doesn't need to be complex. Maybe start by writing down a list of everything you enjoy doing or would like to try that involves physical activity. My list includes activities that fit with my interests (mainly water and the outdoors), level of fitness and capacity, and what is easily accessible to me.
- **Make it enjoyable**. If you feel exercise is a chore, you are likely going to lose motivation. Stick with activities you enjoy doing or consider options that might make exercise more enjoyable, like making it social and inviting a friend.
- **Moderation**. Overexercising is counterproductive. Aim for *regular* (at least three days a week) and *moderate* (at least to the point of huff and puff with an increase in heart rate).
- **Variety and flexibility**. This is where maintaining a list of your exercise activities comes in handy. Having variety prevents exercise from becoming boring, and making it flexible keeps it achievable. From my list of activities, for example, I try to plan three visits to the gym for weight training spread throughout the week. I may plan for the gym on Wednesday, but Wednesday arrives and I don't really feel like the gym. Rather than doing nothing, I'll go to my list and pick something I *am*

in the mood for, maybe something outdoors like a bushwalk, and I'll fit the gym in another day.

- **Set your intention**. I have seen people start exercising because they want to lose weight, which is fine as long as you have strong motivation and self-discipline, because some give up if they don't see quick results. Personally, I prefer to set the intention that I am going out to *exercise my mind and mood.* I set that intention as a reminder of why I'm doing it, and I know that I'll achieve that intention every time I walk out the door to exercise. Besides, when it comes to the physical health benefits, where the mind goes, the body will follow.
- **Capacity**. Exercise within your limits. If you have physical problems through illness or injury, consider talking to a health professional like a doctor or exercise physiologist and get advice on overcoming your limitations, which leads me to my final word on exercise.

▪▪▪

For years I have talked about the benefits of exercise when delivering mental health, wellbeing and resilience talks and courses. There have been occasions where participants will say something like, 'Craig, I can't exercise because I have a bad back', or some other impairment, which may be a fair point, so I usually just share a story about my mate Grant.

Grant is in his mid-forties and lives around the corner from me in Lake Macquarie. He was born with a brain disease called cerebellar ataxia, a serious condition that affects co-ordination, balance, speech and many other motor functions. His disease wasn't diagnosed until age eleven when it was noticed how often Grant fell while running between the wickets at cricket. The disease gradually progressed over time, eventually leading to full wheelchair dependency by age twenty-eight.

In his twenties, Grant developed significant anxiety issues, including a fear of crowds, of trying anything new and even of going anywhere due to a fear of not knowing if accessible facilities like toilets would be available. He didn't tell anyone about those feelings and just battled through. By age thirty-five he commenced a TAFE course in sign-writing, and while that was a positive step, it led him to notice how much his friends were doing with their lives that he was missing out on. Depression soon set in alongside anxiety, leaving Grant feeling down all the time and often irritable. To help cope with depression, Grant ate a lot (commonly referred to as comfort eating), which led to problematic weight gain, and his family became really worried about him. In 2017 they moved north from Sydney to Lake Macquarie for an improved quality of life for Grant.

The real turning point for Grant occurred when his mum, Cheryl, was diagnosed with cancer shortly after the move. Cheryl's cancer was out of Grant's control, but what he could control was easing her worry by turning his own life around. Remembering a mate who had used exercise to recover from depression, Grant decided to join a gym. Finding a gym that is a good personal fit can be difficult, and after trying a few, Grant rolled into my local gym in 2019. He was warmly welcomed and knew immediately he had found the launching pad from which to change his life. With the help of his dad, Steve, and various friends, Grant turned up to the gym four days a week. Under the guidance of his personal trainer, Judie, Grant trained hard and adopted a healthier diet. Sometimes Grant would be at the gym at the same time as me, and I was always moved by his grit and positivity. One day I walked up and introduced myself to Grant, and from there we became close friends and started training together.

Through exercise, Grant fully recovered from depression and anxiety. His recovery happened without medication or psychological therapy. He achieved recovery by taking responsibility for himself, commitment to action, making better choices, having the love and support of his family, and building a strong social network of friends. He also lost around twenty kilograms, and to top it all off, his mother recovered from cancer!

I still pick Grant up from the home he shares with his parents, throw his wheelchair in the back of my ute, and we head to the gym for our workout. Grant never ceases to inspire me, and he does so through his *attitude*.

Grant never asks himself 'what *can't* I do?' – he asks himself 'what *can* I do?' and 'what *could* I do if I ask for help?'

Food for thought.

CHAPTER 8

Mindful connection and meditation

Having set my action for exercise, I turned my mind to how I was going to incorporate the daily practice of mindfulness into my recovery game plan. Before my breakdown I had heard of meditation, but I had never heard the word *mindfulness* nor been introduced to its concepts. To explain what mindfulness is, I often share the story of how my eyes were opened up to it for the first time.

One day very early in my treatment, I attended an appointment with my regular psychologist, Annette. That week had been a bad one for my PTSD and anxiety due to several triggers, and when I walked in the door of Annette's clinic, she could see I was in bad shape. She started by running me through some very simple breathwork to get me a little more settled before saying, 'Craig, I'm going to try something new, but I think you will like it. In a moment, what I'd like you to do is identify and describe to me in detail five things you can see in this room, then five things you can hear and, last of all, five things you can feel against your skin. Then four things you can see, hear and feel. Then three things, two things and then one thing you can see, hear and feel on your body. Let's have a quick practice first.'

In my first run, I said things like 'I can see a clock', 'I can see a painting on the wall', 'I can hear a bird', 'I can feel my shoes', and so on. Then Annette gave me some guidance and I started again. This time I said things like:

'I can see a painting on the wall, and there is a bridge in the painting, and I can see the bridge is supported by one, two, three ... seven pylons.'

'I can see a clock on the wall. It is white, and the second hand is red ...'

'I can hear a bird outside; it sounds like a magpie. It sounds happy ...'

'I can hear a car driving past; it is travelling from my right to my left. It sounds like a small car ...'

'I can feel my left shoe. I can feel the warmth it is creating around my foot and the slight tightness the laces are creating over the top of my foot ...'

'I can feel my sunglasses resting on top of my head. I can feel the arms of the glasses pressing gainst my temples and I can feel the light weight of the frame resting near my hairline ...'

When I finished the exercise, describing five things, four things, all the way down to the last thing I could see, hear and feel, Annette asked me how I was feeling, and the honest answer was ... way better! I was so much calmer. My heart rate had dropped, my breathing had settled and stifling tension had left my body.

The reason I felt way better was that before I engaged in this activity, my entire focus was caught up in all the looping negative thoughts bouncing around in my head and the horrible physical symptoms I was experiencing. But as with most people, my brain doesn't have the capacity to do multiple tasks at once, so when I redirected my brain to identifying and describing in detail the things I could see, hear and feel, all those thoughts and feelings I had been experiencing were shut down. The exercise of tapping into my sensory experiences in the room *in the moment* acted like a circuit breaker for my brain and gave my mind and body a chance to reset. That is mindfulness and meditation, and from that day I was a believer. I called it my 'five to one' meditation practice, and it was good for me because it was practical, I could do it anywhere, and it suited me and my personality. Now back to the game plan.

When considering my action for the recovery strategy of meditation, I thought about how well my five to one worked for me, but I also realised that I wasn't committing to regular practice, so I knew I needed to do more. I took the time to think about how I could build on my five to one and get more out of it by aligning it with my interests. Then it came to me: I love to write. Over those few years I had been sporadically writing a memoir, and I enjoyed the creative experience. I now had my action.

My action for meditation was to build on my five to one by taking my laptop to nice places and writing short descriptive stories about the things I could see, hear and feel in that place at that time. At first I took my laptop on bushwalks in local rainforests, and I could get lost for hours describing in words the sights, sounds and things I could physically feel in the present moment. Here is an example.

The Crossing

My eyes follow the stream. In places, deep pools give the illusion of stillness. In other places, pebbly shallows and small waterfalls reveal otherwise.

The banks are lined with lush rainforest foliage that grows unbroken until it reaches a bridge.

It is an old bridge. Many of the thick wooden planks are rotted, and in places, some have been exchanged for new. The originals, in my mind, are like old teeth.

Some of the teeth are chipped. Some of the teeth have holes. There are gaps left between the teeth from those that have rotted out. The remaining teeth, however, lie strong and defiant. They are old, but they are resolute.

The planks are supported below by two massive parallel hardwoods. They span the high side of one bank to the high side of the other.

The ageless timbers are two feet thick. Burly. Robust. Staunch. I can see they will withstand decay, by way of their immensity, for lifetimes to come.

Above, the sides of the bridge are defined by two more parallel beams. Roughly hewn from two entire trees, they press the planking to the spans below. Thick moss carpets the entire length of each, creating a richly coloured, bright green, decorative corridor.

Here and there the moss shares its host with small subtropical ferns. Together they weigh anchor in the soft cracks and crevices of the rotting beams and give life to something long departed.

The mountain air in this damp ravine is very cold, so my nose and fingertips tell me. It is time to find sunshine.

I turn my back and climb towards it, leaving the bridge to its solemn duty.

I called it 'word art' because I was painting pictures, but with words. Occasionally I booked holiday accommodation on my own and retreated in a creative environment to write. Word art was helping me learn to plug myself into the world around me. It was helping me learn to *take notice*. Over time, regular mindfulness/meditation practice settled my fight-or-flight response and helped me find some much-needed peace. It gave my mind and body a chance to rewire and recover.

I have a busy mind. Sometimes that busyness serves me well, and sometimes it works against me, particularly when I get caught up and trapped on merry-go-rounds of repetitive negative thoughts, ruminating over problems in my past or anticipated problems in my future. Through the regular practice of mindfulness, I trained myself to catch it when stuck in my thoughts, acknowledge it, and then reset my mind by bringing focus back to the world around me in the present moment. Mindfulness can be as simple as this.

Often when I'm exercising, out on my beach or bushwalking, for example, I am in relative solitude, which gives my busy mind plenty of room to take off on its own. I might get stuck ruminating over stressful family problems or work or something from my past or future, and consequently I am missing the beautiful weather, the blue water of the lake, the breeze through the trees. Now, though, my practice means I mostly catch it before it's too late. I might be fifteen minutes into my walk when, without judgement, I acknowledge that I've been caught up in my thoughts and then do something to help me reconnect. Sometimes I pick up a shell on the beach, or pluck a leaf off a tree in the bush, and while I'm walking, without looking at the object, I try to identify and really *notice* what I can feel in my fingertips – the texture, temperature, imperfections, ridges, bumps and anything else I can discern. With my full focus diverted through my sense of touch to that object in that moment, I have tripped a circuit breaker for all my previous ruminations, shutting them down and giving my brain a chance to reset. And because I have taken the time to bring myself back to the present, everything else around me starts to come into focus. I am now plugged into the world around me and enjoy the rest of my walk so much more. That's how easy it can be.

There are so many mindfulness/meditation techniques available, including focusing on breath, five-sense practice (my five to one), body-scan meditations and much more. I recommend trying a variety of practices until you find one that fits best. My mindfulness action was writing, but I know people who use art or colouring in. Many yoga instructors and therapists will guide people through meditation practices, and there are several excellent meditation apps out there. When encouraging others to introduce mindfulness in their lives, there are a few things that I suggest:

- **Seek guidance.** Many counsellors, psychologists, and dedicated meditation practitioners and retreats will provide guidance on how to learn and practise mindfulness. I also highly recommend giving yoga a try, and many yoga instructors incorporate a meditation practice to start and conclude yoga sessions. Some of my most amazing meditation sessions followed a yoga class. Ask for recommendations from people you know who practise meditation.

- **Experiment.** Have a curious mind and research a variety of meditation practices. Download and explore a meditation app like Insight Timer, Smiling Mind or Headspace. Save or write a list of those you find enjoyable and connect with.
- **Practise without judgement.** People often give up on meditation because 'I'm not good at it'. Be kind to yourself. Avoid being self-critical if your mind keeps wandering or you get caught in your thoughts. Just acknowledge it, congratulate yourself for noticing, and come back to your practice.
- **Remember your senses.** What you see, what you hear, what you feel, what you taste, what you smell. Most of us have five senses we can use to come back to the present when we are caught in ruminating thoughts. Tap into them.
- **Make time.** Set a time for meditation and get into a routine. The more regularly you practise, the more you will benefit.

Through mindfulness and meditation, I learned how to take back control of how much time I spend in my own head and how I spend that time when I'm there. And while mindfulness helped me learn to take time out from my thoughts, it was the next strategy that helped me learn how to reshape them.

CHAPTER 9

Challenging negative thinking

Our thoughts and beliefs affect the way we feel and, sometimes, the way we behave. If we have pleasant thoughts then we might feel positive and happy, but negative thoughts will lead to feelings of distress, worry, fear, anger and other negative human emotions.

During my journey through depression and PTSD, my thoughts and beliefs were so overwhelmingly negative that, over time, negative thinking and negative self-talk became my hardwired, default thinking process. Anytime anything went wrong or I faced a challenging situation, my automatic thinking response was negative. The more this happened, the more automatic the behaviour became. Back then, I didn't understand the way the brain works, the way it is structured, and how those structures can change and be influenced. I have learned a lot since, and I'll share some of that knowledge with you shortly, but first, let's go back to my game plan.

Cognitive behaviour therapy (CBT) is used to help people challenge and change unhelpful thinking behaviours. Often used for the treatment of depression, anxiety and other mental health conditions, it works on the basis that the way we think affects the way we feel, which then often affects our behaviours. A few examples of negative-thinking behaviours that CBT can help include:

- **fortune-telling** (predictions of possible bad outcomes, even with no evidence to support them)
- **blaming** (blaming self or others for situations or emotional distress)
- **shoulds** (believing self, others or situations in life *should* or *ought* to be a certain way)
- **catastrophising** (close to fortune-telling but, going further than just predicting bad outcomes, it's being *convinced* that bad outcomes *will* occur without evidence and without considering the possibility of less catastrophic outcomes).

During my initial three years of treatment, my psychiatrist had introduced CBT many times using thought-challenging worksheets to try to change my often-distorted view of situations that caused me distress. I always resisted it, partly because I was stubborn in my beliefs and partly because I couldn't see how worksheets could turn my life around. Maybe if I had understood a little more of how the brain works,

I might have given it more commitment. But sitting in my lounge room that time after a suicide attempt, I knew that regardless of my belief, I needed to give the process full commitment and trust that some benefit would come from it. So I came up with my game plan action for CBT.

I printed out a stack of blank thought-challenging worksheets and divided them into two folders. I placed one folder in my car and one at home next to my bed. My action for CBT was that every time I experienced unpleasant or distressing feelings and emotions, I had to immediately pull out a worksheet and on it:

- identify the way I felt (angry, sad, stressed, worried, et cetera)
- identify the thought or belief that led me to feel that way
- identify and record the evidence that supported the thought or belief
- identify and record the evidence weighted against it
- record a positive action to move forward.

I made a firm commitment to myself that whenever I was triggered, whenever I felt myself getting angry, whenever I felt myself overreacting to a situation, whenever I felt worried or distressed, I would pull out a thought-challenging worksheet on the spot.

Setting up those two folders was a critical ingredient for how CBT worked for me moving forward. Having a worksheet close at hand wherever I was meant I had no excuse to avoid commitment to my action. Even if I had to pull my car over and work on it on the side of the road, I would do it. And because of that hard work and commitment to action, I gradually started to notice changes in the way I was thinking and responding to challenging situations. In fact, one of the earliest examples of this change happened in my car.

I was driving from Coffs Harbour one day and, in a moment of indecision, found myself caught in the wrong lane. The lane I was in would take me very much out of my way, and I was in a hurry to get home. I felt my usual rise in anger and self-criticism begin, but before it took hold, for the very first time I stopped and thought to myself, *Hang on a minute, mate – let's challenge this. Maybe getting caught in this lane could work in your favour. There could be a traffic problem the other way and you may have actually saved time, not lost it. You're in a hurry, but do you really need to be? Is the world going to stop turning because you get home a little later?*

Rather than getting angry, what I now felt was pride and a sense of achievement. This was the first time I really noticed my work with CBT starting to create a change in my thinking behaviours. It was also the first time I caught my negative thoughts and beliefs before they took hold and caused problems. And it was the first time I had challenged them in my head without needing a worksheet. Through practice and commitment to my CBT game plan action, I had trained my brain not only to catch negative thinking earlier but to also rationally work through challenging situations in a much more positive and less emotive way. Getting stuck in the wrong lane turned out to be a blessing.

My work with CBT over many months was not on its own a magic bullet in my eventual recovery, but I truly believe it led to many improvements in the way I think. In a way, *all* my recovery game plan strategies were working together, complementing each other. While using surfing for exercise, I'd often sit on my board in the water and practise mindfulness. Through mindfulness I was learning how to recognise when I was caught in negative thinking and how to bring myself back to the present. Through CBT I was learning how to challenge those negative thoughts. By committing to all these strategies, I was retraining and rewiring my brain though a process I didn't know about then, but I do now. It's called *neuroplasticity*.

I am not a doctor or clinician so I am not going to delve too deeply into the science behind neuroplasticity, but I have learned a lot in recent years through reading scientific literature and attending tutorials. The first time I heard of neuroplasticity – which basically means the ability of the brain to structurally change itself – was soon after my recovery, at a Quest for Life Foundation trauma workshop for former police officers. I was working as a volunteer mentor at the time, and psychotherapist Margie Braunstein was delivering the workshop for our program. Although she didn't talk at length on the subject, what Margie shared about neuroplasticity captured me. Everything about it explained how trauma had changed my brain, but it also explained how the strategies I used in my recovery had worked to change it back.

I don't accept anything at face value, so I set about researching the subject. I listened to podcasts and audiobooks. I read books, including one written by psychiatrist Norman Doidge called *The Brain that Changes Itself*, and the more I learned, the more I needed to learn. I discovered that the theory of neuroplasticity has been around for a long time, but advances in modern research and medical imaging technology have moved the science on from just theory. This is my layman's view on how neuroplasticity worked for me.

I have more neural connections in my mind and throughout my body than there are leaves on trees in the Amazon rainforest. Literally *billions* of them. My actions, behaviours, learning, thinking, memories and much more occur through the creation of neural connections, pathways and networks. When I learn something new, I grow a neural connection. When I repeat it, I form a neural pathway. The more I repeat it, the stronger that neural pathway becomes. On the flip side, pathways that are no longer being used get pruned away, so it's a 'use it or lose it' scenario.

Depression and PTSD had led me down a path of continual negative-thinking behaviours. The neural pathways I had grown from negative responses to just about everything in my life during that time, including negative self-talk and catastrophising, had through repetition grown those neural pathways into *superhighways*. Those superhighways then became my automatic default for how I responded to every challenging situation, large or small, like being stuck driving around and around in circles on an out-of-date road map.

When I started using my thought-challenging worksheets, however, I was growing new neural connections in response to that learning stimulus. Rather than allowing myself to drive straight down my already established thinking superhighways, I was taking the time to grow new thinking pathways that, with repetition, were gradually growing into new roads and, eventually, more positive-thinking superhighways. Those new superhighways became my new automatic default for how I responded to challenging situations in my life, and the old superhighways fell into disrepair through lack of use. This is what my experience felt like. It's not very scientific, but for me, it fits. Worksheet practice helped retrain and *rewire* my brain.

But my work with CBT didn't just help reshape thinking responses to given situations, it also helped me learn one of the most important lessons in my life: the ability to reshape the way I think about all the challenging situations and adversities I face.

▪ ▪ ▪

In the days after my suicide attempt, while I was in my lounge room working on my game plan strategy for challenging negative thinking, I got to thinking about the negative way I had been looking at everything that had happened to me since my medical retirement from the police force.

The first thing I identified was that when people asked me why I wasn't in the police force anymore, or if I explained why I didn't have a job, I would always say something like *I suffer from PTSD*, or *I suffer from depression*. I wrote that word down, 'suffer', and when I looked at it, I realised that every time I used it to describe my situation, I was reinforcing a negative message that I was the victim of my illnesses, which meant my illnesses had control over me. That had to change.

I also considered the fact that I had focused on everything with a sense of loss. I had lost my career. I had lost my identity as a cop, which was my soul. I had lost friendships, my health, my marriage. I had lost the last three years of my life. The way I had been thinking about and speaking about my illnesses was keeping me locked in a *negative victim mindset* of grief and loss. I needed to find a way to turn negative into positive, loss into gain, and not only take back control of my life but make those last three years worth going through. I thought about it and made some decisions.

The first decision was making a commitment to myself never to use the word suffer again. Instead, I would say 'I *live with* PTSD' or 'I *live with* depression'. From that day on, saying I lived with those illnesses helped reinforce a more positive message that my illnesses and I now coexisted, which meant I was no longer their victim, which meant I was taking back control. It also implied *acceptance*, which turned out to be an incredibly important element of my recovery game plan. For three years I had been fighting *against* the symptoms of my illnesses, which constantly led to setbacks. With acceptance I started to work *with* those symptoms, which led to progress.

The second decision was finding a way to turn negative into positive and loss into gain. One way to do that, I thought, would be to share my experiences so others could learn from them, particularly regarding the consequences of not getting early help. For that I needed a platform, but I didn't have one. I thought about raising money for mental health research or services, with the added benefit of using the fundraiser to raise awareness, and I didn't need to think long about how I would do it. A few years earlier I had fallen in love with riding motorcycles, and what better for my recovery than a big, long motorbike ride ... like, right around Australia. The next question was, who will I fundraise for?

Way back at the start of my recovery journey I had used the online self-screening tools of the Black Dog Institute (BDI) and accessed some of their resources. Looking up their website now and reading about the research they were doing into mental health prevention and treatment, I decided then and there to put together a motorbike ride and raise money to help fund those projects. That's how I would turn negative into positive, loss into gain.

For the next couple of days, I worked on a detailed fundraising proposal to send to the Black Dog Institute. During my next appointment with Dr Kramer, I told him about my idea, and fortunately he was able to introduce me by email to a friend, Bridie, who worked at BDI as a psychologist. I emailed my proposal to her that day in the hope that I would soon find myself riding my motorbike around the country on a fundraising and awareness campaign.

What happened, as it turned out, was way better.

CHAPTER 10

Turning a negative into a positive

The day after I sent the email, Bridie called. After a chat, she said, 'Craig, you have an amazing story, and you have articulated it beautifully in your proposal. We have an education program of volunteers with lived experience of mental illness who share their stories in the community and to kids in high schools. If you are interested, I'll put the community education team in touch with you. I think you could be great at this, and we would love to have you on board.'

I needed no time to consider, and the community education team lined me up for a one-day facilitators' workshop in June of 2015. For the three months leading up to the BDI workshop, I committed to my recovery game plan strategies with surfing, meditation through word art, CBT worksheets, bushwalking, yoga classes and weight training at the PCYC gym. I occasionally went away on my own, either camping and fishing in national parks or renting holiday accommodation to give me the freedom to write. In addition to word art, writing about my life experiences in the form of memoir was a game plan strategy from which I gained immense benefit (I'll share more on this in the last chapter).

The Black Dog workshop was held at a function centre in a Coffs Harbour resort, which was convenient for me but did nothing to reduce the anxiety I felt walking in. The facilitator, BDI's Shannon Nolan, was in her thirties, with dark hair and an easy smile, and she welcomed me before I took a seat at a boardroom table. There were close to ten others in the room, all with different lived experiences of mental illness, and all women. I was the only bloke in the whole room, a reflection, maybe, of the difficulties men have in opening up about mental health. For the rest of that day, Shannon led us through the community education program, including visual presentations and basic facilitation skills. We all had an opportunity to stand up front and tell a little of our stories, which gave me an idea of just how difficult it is to share private, personal and emotional information with strangers. I was given an information pack and a USB with PowerPoint slides before heading home to wait for my first presentation opportunity.

A couple of weeks after the workshop, I accepted my first booking for a high school presentation. Of all places it was the local high school, my kids' school, Woolgoolga High. It was a few weeks away, so I used the time to prepare my presentation slides and practise talking through it. However, the closer I came to presentation day, the more anxious I became, and by the time the day arrived, I was terrified.

The presentation from BDI was called 'Breaking Down Depression and Building Resilience', a combination of educational slides with my story woven in. My task that day was to deliver the one-hour presentation to one hundred and seventy Year 9 and 10 students in two back-to-back afternoon sessions. I drove the short distance from home to the school, pulled into the teachers' car park and just sat there, hands tightly clasped on the steering wheel of my four-wheel drive ute, totally petrified. I've done some scary stuff in my time – a lot of dangerous, risky stuff. I've entered burning houses, fought bad men, kicked down doors and all sorts of other things, but honestly, none of that scared me as much as the impending reality of standing in front of one hundred and seventy high-school kids and opening up about my personal life. It was still so raw and emotional, and for a bit of added pressure, my son Owen was going to be in the audience for the first session along with all his friends. I was so very close to reversing my ute out and driving home, but I didn't. I reminded myself why I was doing it, grabbed my laptop, got out of the car and walked into the school.

I was in the library setting up when the first session of kids started rolling in, with all the noisy banter, laughter and loud conversation you'd expect from dozens of teenagers. Owen and some of his mates came up and wished me luck, which helped settle the nerves a little. The head teacher took care of introductions and then I just jumped straight into it. I was nervous, the presentation wasn't polished, but I got through. The kids were great, tuned in and respectful, and as they were leaving, something unexpected happened. I was busy resetting my presentation for the next group when I looked up and saw that maybe seven or eight young men and women were lined up in front of me.

The first, a young man of about sixteen, shook my hand and thanked me, then he shared his diagnosis of depression and what it was like for him to live with that as an adolescent. Fifty percent of people who experience depression have their first episode before the age of eighteen, so there are a lot of kids out there doing it tough. Next a young woman around the same age shared her battle with anxiety. Some of the others told me of their parents' struggles with mental health problems, and some asked questions on how to help a friend. Somewhere in all this my son came over, shook my hand and congratulated me. Then a second group of seventy kids shuffled in and I delivered the presentation again, and once more, when I finished, kids lined up to have a chat. As much as I was proud of myself for managing to survive those very first presentations, it was this personal interaction afterwards that really struck me. Thinking about it later, I realised that seeing this tough ex-cop get up and allow himself to be *vulnerable* made me approachable to these kids, like they knew I would get them and understand what they were going through. For me, that was very special. I walked out of Woolgoolga High School that day way taller than when I walked in because I had just taken a first step in turning my negative experiences into something more positive.

Those two presentations opened my eyes to the power of shared lived experience. They also demonstrated how mentally, emotionally and physically draining it is to relive trauma in the telling of my story, so I decided I needed to be careful in how much I took on. I had one or two more bookings at high schools in Coffs Harbour towards the end of 2015, but other than that, there were very few requests, and I wasn't sure where it was all heading. In hindsight, that was probably a good thing, because it allowed me time to work on my recovery and rebuild my resilience. And I was going to need that because my work with BDI wasn't staying quiet for long.

In early 2016, Shannon called me from BDI. 'Hey, mate. We're getting some requests for presentations to rural communities and schools out west. The feedback from your presentations is fantastic, and I think you'd be the perfect fit out there. Are you okay to travel?'

I laughed. 'Shannon, I have a motorbike – absolutely I'll travel!'

From there, BDI teamed up with the Rural Adversity Mental Health Program (RAMHP) and organised a week-long tour of the New South Wales Central West region. I called up my good mate and former Coffs Harbour detective Trevor Walter. Trev put thirty-seven years into the police force before his retirement and in 2011 was awarded a commissioner's award for outstanding victim care. He was also one of the nicest blokes I knew, and like me, he loved getting away on his motorbike. Trev and I had a trip to plan: a motorbike tour with a purpose.

CHAPTER 11

Finding meaning and purpose

Riding a motorbike is a mindful experience, and I was right there in the moment. Trev was just ahead of me, and I could see him diving into the winding mountain road with as much excitement as I was. We were riding up the Waterfall Way, Coffs Harbour's gateway to the west, through the ancient World Heritage rainforest of the Dorrigo National Park, and through meditation, at times like these I had learned to take notice.

To my left, cascading waterfalls washed down towering rock faces before vanishing under the road beneath me. To my right, prehistoric tree ferns, palms and other rainforest flora framed majestic escarpments that stood vigil over the Bellingen valley hundreds of metres below. It was so beautiful, and I felt totally connected.

West of the Great Divide, with perfectly clear weather on our side, we rode out through the Northern Tablelands, down through Tamworth and Werris Creek, and after six hours in the saddle we pulled into a one-pub town called Tambar Springs. The warm, friendly hospitality extended to Trev and I that evening, typical of country people, reinforced one of the main reasons I had jumped at the chance to take on this tour of the Central West.

Rural communities are full of tough, self-reliant, proud people who generally give more than they ask. When times are tough, they tend to grin and battle on. I also know, from experience, that it is this admirable pride and self-reliance that can leave rural people vulnerable to the sometimes tragic consequences of untreated mental health problems. As a young detective I attended the scene of my first farmer suicide soon after transferring to outback Hay in 1993. Unfortunately it wasn't my last, and no matter how much I tried then, I could never truly understand it. Now, sitting on my motorcycle, armed with insight courtesy of my own journey through mental illness, I was heading back out there. Not to Hay this time, but to towns just like it.

Trangie, Parkes, Kandos, Mudgee and Blayney. We rode to five country towns in five days. After delivering a talk at one school I was on the bike travelling to the next, sometimes delivering additional evening talks to parents or community groups. I shared my story with more than a thousand kids and parents over those five days – a significant challenge, particularly back in those early days of my recovery.

I have had so many people approach me after delivering lived-experience talks, often people with their own histories of mental illness asking how they could get a start doing the same thing. I am always supportive and offer pathways, but I also prepare them for how hard it is to get up and share your life with crowds of strangers. Friends and family who have seen me speak publicly tell me I make it look easy, but that's what they see on the outside. The inside often looks and feels much different. The telling of my story also involves *reliving* it, and the most important parts tend to invoke the strongest internal feelings and emotions. These days I manage those challenges with a strong sense of *self-awareness* and a high degree of *self-care*. On that first tour, though, to help me get through, I had the company and support of my mate Trev.

Trev could see how exhausted I was after each presentation, so to give me time to decompress, he took the lead in getting me safely to the next town, every day for the whole five days. He organised fuel stops, planned our next route and on a couple of occasions sat up on the stage with me. I couldn't have done it without him, and I mean that literally, because the whole tour nearly met disaster on day two.

I had just finished delivering a presentation to more than three hundred kids at Parkes High School, the largest audience I had ever addressed, and I was very tired. I locked my laptop in one of the side panniers of my bike, kitted up and followed Trev out of Parkes towards the Bylong Valley town of Kandos. We rode for at least an hour before stopping at a small-town service station for fuel, and when I stepped off my bike, I immediately saw a big problem: one of my side panniers, the hard luggage cases that contained all my belongings, had fallen off. Panic set in. I hurriedly unlocked the remaining pannier in the hope it contained my laptop, but I knew before I opened it that I wasn't going to be that lucky. My laptop and all the backed-up USBs that were with it were gone. Three years of hard, often emotional work writing my journals and memoirs along with all the PowerPoint presentations for the school tour. I couldn't believe it. I was completely devastated not only by the loss of so much of my recorded life but also by the realisation that I had let down the Black Dog Institute and the schools that were booked in for the next three days. It was all over before it really began. But Trev would hear nothing of it.

'Come on, Semps,' he said. 'We'll backtrack and look for it all the way back to Parkes if we have to, mate. We'll find it.'

With tears running down my face, I tried to explain the futility of a search to Trev. We had just travelled over a hundred kilometres from Parkes along a road almost entirely free of other motorists that was closely lined on either side with dense scrub and bushland. Coming off my bike at around a hundred kilometres an hour, the pannier would have been launched clear of the road into the surrounding bush, where its blackness would make it near impossible to see. There was no chance of recovering it. I had given up, but not Trev. He jumped on his bike and started off back down the road towards Parkes. Having little choice, I got back on my bike and followed.

We rode slow, around twenty or thirty k's an hour, with Trev looking into the bush on one side of the road and me the other. Even brightly coloured rubbish was hard to spot in the roadside scrub. Every now and then I yelled out that this was hopeless and we should go back, but Trev kept pushing me on.

After searching for nearly two heartbreaking hours, we rounded a corner and saw a small shoulder cleared of bush ahead, just big enough to park a car or two. It was the only patch of scrub-free roadside on the entire stretch we had covered, and sitting smack in the middle of it was my luggage pannier! I couldn't believe it. The chance of the pannier landing in the middle of the only small clearing along a hundred kilometres of road was just too hard to conceive.

We raced our bikes over and found it was largely intact, and when I opened it to find my laptop undamaged, Trev and I hugged and danced and laughed so hard I couldn't breathe. The pair of us would have made a bewildering sight to anyone driving past, but we didn't care. It was the most unbelievable stroke of luck that was as close to a true miracle as I have ever experienced. Our celebrations were cut a little short, though, as the pannier had not only landed in a clearing but also on top of a large bull ant nest, and our jumping around brought them on the attack in their hundreds. We jumped on our bikes and rode to Kandos, me cheering loudly all the way.

I can't think of any other time in my life where I have gone from such utter despair to incredible happiness and elation than that moment, and that's part of the reason I'll never forget it. The other part is that Trev's hope and optimism, at a time when there was no reason to have any, has served as an important lesson for me to reflect on at times of significant adversity.

No matter how tough life becomes or how hopeless a situation might seem, never *ever* give up!

▪▪▪

I delivered my final presentation to the kids at Blayney High School on the last day of the tour, and as we rode out of town, with Trev again in the lead, I took some time to appreciate the week's experiences. I reflected that in addition to the respect and courtesy extended from these kids, I was most astounded by their levels of engagement and comprehension. Proof of that comprehension was demonstrated by the overwhelmingly mature questions asked by so many of them at the end of each talk, and by so many kids approaching me afterwards to offer thanks or to share their personal stories. And when kids told me stories of how they were battling through their own experiences with personal or family mental health problems, when they told me about losing a teenage friend to suicide, it was all I needed to know that what I was doing was so worthwhile.

That first tour would never have happened nor been the success it was without the tireless efforts of a truly remarkable woman from Canowindra, Di Gill. Di was the Rural Adversity Mental Health Program co-ordinator for the Central West, and I am yet to meet a person more passionate and dedicated to the wellbeing of farmers and rural communities. Di organised and supported each of the presentations throughout that week, and because the tour went so well, it wasn't long before she organised another one. And after that, Di invited me out to speak at rural events, expos, agricultural awards nights and more. Somewhere in among all this, BDI received a grant to send me over to Western Australia, and I toured the wheat belt for a week, speaking to kids in remote schools.

I loved it all. The more talks I delivered, the stronger I became, and at some point, after about a year of all these speaking engagements, I recognised I had reached a turning point in my recovery. That turning point wasn't some magic moment where suddenly I was well again, it was simply the point where, for the first time in many years, I was having more good days than bad. My interactions with all those thousands of schoolkids were not only refilling my emotional bucket, they were also filling my heart.

My work with BDI was helping me heal in so many ways, not least of which was the fact that I was doing it as a volunteer.

CHAPTER 12

The healing power of giving back

The first time I genuinely experienced the healing power of *giving* through volunteer work was during the final seven years of my police career. At the time I was a member of the New South Wales Police Surfing Association, and through another member I was introduced to the Disabled Surfers Association of Australia (DSA).

The DSA is a volunteer organisation that supports people with a broad range of intellectual and physical disabilities and injuries (including cerebral palsy, Parkinson's disease, multiple sclerosis, Down syndrome, paraplegia and many more) enjoy the thrill of riding a wave to shore on a surfboard. There are nineteen chapters around the country, and thousands of volunteers support them. We had a local mid-north coast chapter that held summer surfing events around the region.

I didn't know what to expect when I attended my first event in Coffs Harbour, but it certainly wasn't to be as profoundly affected as I was. For three hours straight I saw participants falling off, then volunteers pulling them up out of the water, coughing and spluttering, so they could get back on and do it again. I saw participants cheering each other on and challenging each other. I saw participants conquering their fears. I saw the deepest display of trust I have ever witnessed from people knowing their lives depended on helping hands being there when they needed them. Most of all, I saw so much *laughter*! I had never seen a purer form of joy on a human face, and it was impossible not to be infected with that joy.

Likewise, I saw volunteers laughing and having fun. I saw them working as a team and building camaraderie. I even saw a few, including me, wipe away tears shed not from sadness but from the happiness experienced in bringing such immense joy to the lives of others. Afterwards, everyone gathered for a barbecue and some fun award presentations, and when I finally arrived home, having spent three hours lifting and pulling and wading back and forth through the surf, I collapsed on my couch and fell into the most satisfyingly exhausted afternoon sleep.

I was so infected by this outpouring of generosity and the feeling of contributing to a joint sense of community purpose that I became a regular, progressing to a volunteer team leader. I didn't know it then but every time I attended a DSA surfing event, I was benefiting as much or more than the actual participants I was helping. Professionally, I was drowning in stress and working in a violent, often negative environment. But the positive emotions I experienced at DSA helped provide balance and boosted my wellbeing. I developed strong social networks surrounded by positive people.

Volunteering with DSA gave me a better sense of meaning, purpose and *perspective*, which brings me back to my volunteer work with the Black Dog Institute years later.

■■■

Some of the interactions I had with those thousands of schoolkids were life-changing, not just for them but also for me. I had so many incredible moments during the years sharing my story with these kids, but there are two that stand out.

After delivering a talk to about a hundred and sixty kids at a regional high school, I was approached by a young woman about fourteen years of age. With a bright personality and emotional intelligence well beyond her years, she shared her struggles living with anxiety, but importantly, she also shared her positive outlook for the future. One part of her experience with anxiety that troubled her, though, was a belief that her dad, her loving and caring sole parent, couldn't understand the impact of her anxiety problems, as hard as he tried. This kid really touched my heart, so I suggested she invite her dad to the parents' presentation I was delivering that night, which she agreed to do, but in all honesty, she didn't think he would come. So that night, before my talk started, I kept scanning the audience and looking to the door hoping to see him, but the few men present were with partners, not obviously sole parents. I delayed the talk for a while but still they were a no show. Sadly, I gave up and began.

I was a few minutes into my presentation when the rear door of the school hall opened. I looked up to see that bright young lady walk in, a smile from ear to ear as she led her father inside. She was holding his hand, and I could tell right away that he was a good dad. They sat down and she held his hand through the entire hour or so that I spoke. I talked about the signs and symptoms of depression and anxiety that were particularly relevant to youth. I shared my own experience, the way I was affected and the impact of my illness on the lives of those close to me, but also positive messages of hope and recovery.

Afterwards, they waited patiently while some other parents approached me for a chat, and then, when they had a chance, the young lady proudly introduced me to her dad. He shook my hand and thanked me. I mean, he truly and warmly *thanked* me. He told me that, for the very first time, he genuinely understood his daughter's experiences in a way that he never had before. I knew he meant it; I could see it through the tears in his eyes. I had the impression it was a defining moment for this man and his relationship with his daughter. We talked for a while and then I watched them leave, him with a protective arm around her all the way out the door. I'm not too tough to admit that, on later reflection, this moment moved me to tears. It still does. It probably stands as one of the most important presentations I have delivered, not because of my ability to speak but because of that good man's ability to *listen*.

On another occasion I spoke at a country high school and, as usual, shared information and personal insight into the topic of suicide. While I was talking to a group of kids afterwards, I noticed a male student hanging back, waiting for the others to finish. When the last of them walked off he approached, shook my hand and introduced himself. He said, 'Craig, I *really* want to thank you for today.'

'You're welcome,' I said, 'but why's that?'

'Well, when I was two years old, my mum killed herself. For my whole life I have been angry at her for doing that and leaving me on my own. But after listening to you, I think I'm starting to understand what she must have been going through.'

'Mate, I'm so sorry about your mum,' I said. 'You did very well to sit through my talk, and I'm glad you did. How are you feeling now?'

He looked me in the eye and calmly replied, 'I think I now feel at peace, Craig.'

And he *was* at peace, I could see it. He shook my hand again and off he walked to his next class.

I cannot find words that do justice to how that interaction made me feel that day, but I can say this. If what transpired between that young man and me was the *only* experience I had from sharing my personal story with so many kids, then he alone would have made my mental health battles totally worth going through. Because for this young man to let go of his anger and resentment towards his lost mother and find peace and forgiveness, well, who knows what a difference that made to his future. And I was only one of over a hundred volunteers, all over the country, who were delivering these programs for BDI. How many lives had they changed ... and saved?

▪ ▪ ▪

Travelling and speaking at schools and to community groups and sharing my experience for the good of others probably had the most profound influence on my eventual recovery for the following reasons:

- As a volunteer, I could safely engage in work at my own pace, with minimal expectations and demands.
- I became much more socially connected, meeting hundreds of people in my travels.
- I was able to safely challenge myself.

- In helping others, I was gaining perspective on my own situation.
- I developed a new and deep sense of purpose and *belief* in myself.

Allow me to expand on that last point. During my police career, I had an immense sense of meaning and purpose and a deeply embedded professional identity. After medical retirement, I had neither. Working as a volunteer gave me something to look forward to. It gave me a reason to get out of bed in the morning. It gave me a new sense of meaning and purpose, and through this I also started to build a new and equally worthy identity from which I reclaimed a sense of personal pride and self-esteem.

From my own experience, I have become so convinced of the healing power of *giving back* that I have sought out research and studies on the subject from around the world, and chief among them was a research paper by Professor Stephen Post entitled 'It's Good to be Good' (he has also published a book on the subject, *Why Good Things Happen to Good People*). Extensive research has proved that, in addition to many other benefits, people who volunteer feel happier, have fewer chronic illnesses, enjoy better mental health and social connections, and have an improved sense of meaning and purpose in their lives.

With all this in mind, finding a way to give back is a great strategy for reducing feelings of helplessness and loss resulting from life's challenges and adversities. It has been for me. Extending an act of kindness to someone who needs it not only helps them, but it also helps us feel better for the giving. Which leads me now to the final, life-changing strategy in my recovery game plan: practising *gratitude*.

CHAPTER 13

Gratitude

Earlier in this book I mentioned my lack of commitment to some of the treatments and therapies I had been introduced to during those first three years of illness, often due to a lack of belief. Included in those were any therapies centred around the practice of *gratitude.* That lack of belief was compounded first by not having knowledge of how the brain works, and second by some poor experiences.

One of those poor experiences occurred during three months of weekly sessions at a Sydney clinic. My homework that week was to go out and look for people performing acts of kindness or doing nice things for others. When asked what I thought would be a realistic number of kind acts to see in a day if I was looking for them, I replied, 'I don't know, maybe fifteen?' The psychologist chuckled and suggested that we keep it a small number, maybe three. So that week

I went out looking for people being kind to others, but unfortunately what happened was I only noticed people who I thought might be doing *bad* things. No one considered that I had been hardwired over two and a half decades to look for and identify bad people, so when I went out looking for examples of good deeds, all I saw was suspicious behaviour. The result back then was that I considered theories like gratitude to be fluffy, feel-good, hippie stuff that had no hope of contributing anything meaningful to my improvement. Thankfully, someone opened my eyes to the power of gratitude before it was too late, and it happened during the BDI facilitators' workshop at Coffs Harbour in 2015.

Remember, this was only a few months after my suicide attempt and early in my recovery game plan. There were ten of us in the room learning to be lived-experience educators, nine of them women. At the end of the day, Shannon, the facilitator from BDI, said in closing, 'I'm going to go around the table and invite each of you to say one thing, just one, that you are grateful for in having a mental illness. I'll give you a minute to think before we start.'

I was astonished. Three months earlier I'd tried to take my life. In the minute she gave us, all I could think of was, *What the hell is she talking about? Does she have any idea what I've been through over the last three years?* With that attitude, it's lucky she didn't pick me to go first, but as she went around the table, these courageous women without hesitation shared what they were grateful for in their experience with mental illness, and slowly, I started to get it. It would have been hard *not* to be inspired. Some of these women had been through or were going through hell, and if they could find things to be grateful for then surely so could I. By my turn, it came to me just in time, and I said, 'You know, Shannon, I'm grateful for my mental illness because it has given me a chance to reconnect and rebuild my relationship with my three sons.' Bang!

Until that moment, I had never given this any thought, but while I was listening to the others, I started thinking about my kids. As much as it wasn't all doom and gloom and I didn't see myself as a failure as a dad, I did have to admit that my kids didn't get the best of me, particularly in the last five years of my police career. I was more often cranky, irritable, with a short fuse, a big drinker and overcommitted to my job. But as much as my mental health battles were tough on my boys, at least we had time together. I drove them to school every day, not because I had to but because I *wanted to*. We played touch footy together in our local comp. I took them on holidays. I rode dirt bikes with them, and I made them the best gourmet sandwiches to be found anywhere on the high school playground (so good, in fact, that my youngest, Niam, made money from selling them to other kids and then bought junk, but that's another story!). Was I grateful for my mental illness that I now had a better relationship with my three sons? Absolutely yes! And I felt so positive after that realisation.

Shannon didn't know it then but she made a lifelong friend out of me from that simple, life-changing activity. On the twenty-minute drive home I started thinking of other things for which I was grateful, like the fact that as much as I loved my job, I was glad that my mental illness meant I no longer had to go around and pick up the pieces from the worst of humanity. I arrived home full of excitement and rifled through my folders of homework. I came across the practice of gratitude through journaling and thereafter added another strategy to my recovery game plan.

I started simply, just placing a notepad and pen next to my bed and, before going to sleep each night, I wrote down three things I was grateful for from the day. Not big, significant events, just little things, like someone backing off and letting me change lanes in traffic, or someone making me laugh or lifting my mood when I was struggling. Before gratitude practice, someone being courteous in traffic may have earned them a little wave but otherwise would have largely been missed. Now, through the learning stimulus of gratitude journaling, I was creating new *neural connections* in my brain for that behaviour. Commitment to action with journaling turned those connections into *pathways*, and the more I noticed to be grateful for, the stronger those pathways became. Over a short period of time, I had trained my brain not only to notice those courtesies in traffic but to stop and appreciate them in the moment. And because I notice how good I feel when someone shows that courtesy to me, I try to pay that courtesy forward to others. If the whole world practised gratitude, it would be a much nicer place.

As a cop who spent most of my working life dealing with the worst of humanity, it is easy to understand how I may have developed such negative and cynical attitudes to the world and everyone in it, belief systems that became hardwired. Depression has that effect too. But gratitude practice helped me to rewire my belief systems and become much more optimistic. There are so many daily experiences now that make me stop and fully appreciate the moment. Even on my bad days, noticing a few good things helps balance out the negatives, and it all started with my game plan strategy of gratitude journaling. Getting back to Shannon's question, the greatest thing that I am now grateful to my mental illness for is making me a better person.

Before my psychological collapse, as I have already shared, I wasn't the nicest person to live with. And although I never want to experience it again, one thing depression did was rip me right back to bare bones, which then provided me with an opportunity to rebuild myself into a better man than I was before. I am so much more empathetic and compassionate than I have ever been. Am I grateful for my experience with mental illness now that I'm a better bloke? You bet!

▪ ▪ ▪

I have shared my experience with practising gratitude, but I have also had the pleasure of witnessing its healing power in many others. Of those, two stories stand out.

A few years ago I delivered a string of mental health, wellbeing and resilience workshops to employees of a federal government organisation, concluding the full-day sessions with a discussion about gratitude. At one of those sessions, as always, I asked the group if anyone in the room has ever practised gratitude journaling, and out of twenty participants, one hand went up. The woman, at the lower end of middle age, was willing to share her experience. She briefly told of her battle with severe depression a few years earlier and that although she had a supportive professional therapist, nothing, including antidepressants, seemed to help. Then a friend suggested gratitude journaling. On her first try, lying in bed with a diary and pen, she was so depressed that she could find nothing to be grateful for, so she simply wrote, *I am grateful that I am still alive*. The next night was the same, as was the next. On the fourth night she repeated the line, but then she added one more. And the next night she added more again. She said, 'Craig, every night I still write in my gratitude journal, but these days I have to make myself stop because now there are so many things I notice to be grateful for.'

Sharing her story in the training room that day, she told us that gratitude journaling was the primary strategy that had lifted her out of the deep trough of depression and helped get her life back. The research backs it, this wonderful woman backs it and, given the positive impact gratitude had on my own recovery, I back it too.

■ ■ ■

During the severe drought that ravaged eastern Australia between 2017 to 2019, two wonderful women named Catherine and Natasha were working with Uniting, a charity that organised several 'pamper days' for remote outback communities. The idea was to get wellbeing services from large regional cities to travel to these satellite communities, set up in the one place for an entire day and provide services for free. In the evening, the entire community was invited to a social dinner, and I was asked if I would volunteer my time to travel out and share my story, including tips for wellbeing, during the dinner event. I jumped at the opportunity.

The first events were held over consecutive days at Hermidale and Carinda, both small rural outposts of about two hundred people in the north-west of New South Wales. The 1400-kilometre round trip from my new home near Newcastle provided plenty of opportunity for me to reflect on why I volunteered. Working as a cop in regional New South Wales for two decades, I had seen droughts before, been caught in suffocating dust storms, but I had never seen such complete destruction of the Australian landscape and everything in it. It was *absolute*. For long distances the only reminders that life ever existed out there were the bones of dead animals, bleached white by the blazing sun. There were moments where, looking through the windows of my air-conditioned four-wheel drive, it didn't seem real, so I would pull to the side of the road and walk along stock fences just to get a sense of it all. Not a blade of grass, barely even a weed. No living thing in sight, just a faint odour of decaying livestock wafting on the hot dry breeze and cracked earth underfoot. In a word, it was Armageddon.

As I drove, I could only imagine the impact on the lives of the individuals and communities who existed out there, but I was soon to hear those stories of devastation and loss firsthand. During the day and later that night, I met and spoke with so many incredibly stoic people who shared personal stories of terrible circumstance that, through their survival, defined for me the true meaning of resilience. Hairdressers, massage therapists, yoga and meditation instructors, beauticians and others set up spaces in the community halls for farmers to come in from the land and be pampered, free of charge. As much as they enjoyed being pampered, though, the underlying intention of the event was to bring them all together for social connection, and from the smiles and laughter, from the looks of peace and relaxation on faces during meditation, that intention was achieved.

In the evening, Uniting staff and local volunteers laid out a wonderful dinner, and towards the end of it I was handed a microphone and invited to speak. At the conclusion of my one-hour talk I shared the story of how practising gratitude had enhanced my life, and I found myself asking a completely unplanned question: 'Can anyone think of anything to be grateful for regarding the drought you're currently experiencing?'

As soon as the words come out of my mouth, I thought, *What have I done?* I'd just asked a hundred men and women – cattle and sheep farmers in the middle of losing everything they owned, many with farms handed down over generations, people who'd had to kill their livestock or give it away – if they could find anything to be grateful for in that experience. It was a risky question, and in the silence that followed, I started to worry. But then a hand was raised, and a woman, senior in years, said, 'Craig, if it wasn't for the drought, we wouldn't be having this wonderful evening here tonight.'

Wow. I was so grateful, first that this lovely woman had saved me, but then because in making that statement, she sowed a seed. Another hand went up, this time a middle-aged man, weathered from a lifetime working in the sun, who said, 'Craig, I've seen the nicest acts of kindness and charity during this drought, and I'm grateful for that.' Then another hardened cattle farmer raised his hand and said, 'Mate, when times are good and we are all doing well, we tend to be looking after ourselves and doing our own thing. Something I have noticed is that this drought has brought us all closer together as a community. I think we sort of needed it, and I am grateful for that.'

I have shared the story of these farmers with thousands of people since, because if these people, right in the middle of one of the most tragic adversities of their lives, could find something to be grateful for from the experience, then surely so can all of us. And if we can find things to be grateful for in our adversities, it helps make them less *adverse*.

CHAPTER 14

Rings of recovery

I have mentioned the turning point in my journey of recovery, but I need to be clear that it was not all plain sailing. I didn't make a simple positive affirmation and suddenly the sun came out. I had a lot of setbacks.

My setbacks mostly consisted of relapses into depression but also some bad periods of anxiety with PTSD. The triggers varied, but regardless of the triggers, these setbacks were dangerous times for me. Any one of them had the potential to derail all the hard work I was putting in. During one of my first setbacks, I was parked in my car on the Woolgoolga headland, bawling my eyes out and terrified that I was falling back into the hell of depression all over again. Then a thought occurred to me: *You've been here before, Craig. Worse than this even. You managed to work your way free of it then, and you'll work your way free of it now. Just let it be what it is. Let it be and it will pass. Go home and do something physical.*

And so I did. I drove home, which was now a ten-acre property just south of Woolgoolga, and put on some work clothes. I walked outside and tried to think of something to do that might lift my mood, and then I saw a tree stump sitting stubbornly in the ground in front of me. There were a lot of stumps around that I had intended to pull out with my tractor, but I walked to the shed, returned with an axe and took my first swing. Then another. I swung that axe for about an hour, completely absorbed in the physicality and mindful concentration of my aim. When I finished, dripping sweat and covered in dirt, I felt so much better having released all that nervous, horrible energy, but also because, right there at my feet, was one of the many tree stumps that needed removing from our property. The relief I experienced from the physical exertion combined with a sense of achievement was quite profound, so much so that from then on, whenever my mood started to slide, I grabbed my axe and chopped out another stump!

What I have learned is that a recovery journey free of relapse is unrealistic. In fact, I encourage anyone on a recovery journey to expect relapses, because if you don't expect them, you won't be prepared for them, and if you're not prepared, they will hit you harder. What I did with those tree stumps was simply return to a small, achievable action for a short period of time, and by doing so I avoided surrender.

I guess my recovery could best be described as a

story of two steps forward, one step back. Whenever I fell back a step, I doubled down on my game plan and took another two steps forward. It was hard work, but it was totally worth it because about two years into my game plan, I could now confidently say I had reached a point of recovery. This is what that meant for me.

First, I was no longer clinically depressed. After five long years, I had reached a point where I had been free of relapse for long enough that, without doubt, I no longer lived with major depressive disorder. Second, I had reached a point of *recovery* from PTSD. What I mean by recovery is that while I still lived with some symptoms of PTSD, I had rewired my mind and body to the point where those symptoms no longer had a significant impact on my ability to function in everyday life. I grabbed hold of that achievement with both hands and ran with it, going from strength to strength and rebuilding my *resilience* in the process.

Resilience has become a bit of a buzzword these days, but regarding mental health and wellbeing, my favourite description of resilience is the one I used during the BDI school talks: 'Resilience is our ability to face the challenges we will confront in our lives, overcome them, and then to come out the other side stronger.' For me, rebuilding my resilience was about facing my mental health adversity and putting strategies in place to overcome it, with those strategies becoming learned behaviours that I now fall back on when I face other adversities in my life. That, for me, is resilience.

Years ago, during a boxing session with one of my sparring partners, I had trained so hard that I didn't think I could go on, and then he said something that stuck with me. 'Semps, I had a trainer who once told me that at the point of total exhaustion, where you can barely lift your gloves, you still have fifteen percent left in you,' he said. 'You just have to find a way to tap into that fifteen percent.' I have often thought back to those words when reflecting on my mental health and recovery journey. The way I see it, at the point when I attempted suicide, I thought I had no resilience left, but in fact, there was still a little bit left in the tank. I just had to find a way to tap into it, which I did, and then I built on it through commitment to psychological, behavioural and lifestyle changes.

The World Health Organization (WHO) defines mental health as 'a state of mental well-being that enables people to cope with the stresses of life, realise their abilities, learn well and work well, and contribute to their community'. What I like about this definition is that it sets a reasonably achievable goal for people living *with* mental health problems to work towards. There is nothing in that definition that says an individual needs to be symptom-free to meet it – in fact, many people living with mental health problems may do so for their lifetime. I believe it's achievable to live with mental health problems and still meet the

WHO definition of mental *health*. For me, recovery is not about being free of mental health problems – it's about learning to live with them better.

Regarding trauma, for example, I don't pretend that all the traumatic events in my life no longer affect me; they do, and they probably always will to some degree. But that's okay with me because I have learned to live with those experiences to the point where they have minimal impact on my ability to cope with the stressors of life, realise my abilities, learn well and work well, and contribute to my community.

▪▪▪

Recovery outcomes for those living with mental health problems are influenced by many factors that fit within what I call 'rings of recovery'. The outer ring, the one that surrounds, protects and encourages the recovery process, is the role *others* have in a person's recovery journey. The inner ring, the one from where real change will take place, is the role the *individual* has in their own recovery, and at its core are the essential ingredients for recovery: hope and belief. I'll share some of my thoughts on each, starting with the outer ring.

Outer ring: Meaningful professional help

Effective, meaningful professional help is reliant on the clinician being a good fit for the person seeking help, and on treatment being tailored to that individual.

Psychologists, psychiatrists, psychotherapists and counsellors all have varying approaches to treatment, so it is not a one-size-fits-all model.

I have seen so many people, including me, give up early on professional help because they didn't feel the clinician understood them or their problems. Rapport and trust are critical to the individual's ongoing engagement with their clinician and treatment strategies, so it is important that if the clinician does not feel like the right fit, the individual should consider asking for a referral to another. Clinicians have a responsibility with this as well, and if they do not feel like they are the best suited for a particular person or underlying problem, they should be honest about it and help the person find someone more appropriate.

Some people may be best served by a team approach, like I was with both a psychiatrist and a psychologist working with me in different but co-ordinated ways. These days, when I feel it's time to offload or seek guidance, my preference is for my psychotherapist, because his 'whole person', non-medical approach is the best fit for me at this point. But as important as it is for the clinician to be the right fit, meaningful professional treatment is a two-way street, and the person seeking treatment needs to give the clinician and treatment strategies a fair go. When it comes to the prescription of medications, however, I encourage people to do their own research, get a second opinion if they hold concerns, and remember that antidepressants don't make people 'anti-depressed' – behavioural and lifestyle changes and good therapy do.

Before moving on from the topic of professional help, there is one important point to make: the earlier someone with mental health problems gets the professional help they need, the better their outcomes will be. Generally, the longer a person experiencing mental problems puts off getting help, the worse those problems will become. In my own experience, for example, if I had sought professional help at the first warning sign that I had a problem with PTSD, my nightmares, I could probably have had it all sorted out in just a few sessions with the right clinician. Because I didn't, in addition to losing my career, health and marriage, I ended up attending more than two hundred and fifty sessions with many clinicians over many years. That's a big difference. One of the main motivations for me sharing my story in talks all over the country is to encourage others to seek help early. The way I often describe it is this: the further and harder we run from mental health problems, the harder we get pulled down in the end. Putting your hand up and asking for help is not a sign of weakness but a sign of strength and courage, and the job for the rest of us is to rally and support others in that process. Which leads me to the second part of the outer ring.

Outer Ring: Support of family and friends

My advice to carers

I am often approached by people desperate for answers about how they can better support a loved one experiencing mental health problems, and the short answer I usually give them is: *ask your loved one what it is they need from you.*

It is important not to assume what that person needs in support or to try and *fix* things for them. By simply asking what they need, you are first showing you care, and second giving them some sense of control over how they will be supported. Try asking something like, 'Craig, when your moods are low or when your anxiety is bad, what is it that you would like me to do to support you?' And Craig might reply, 'Just give me some space for a while, or just give me a hug. That's all.'

It is common for those living with mental health problems to distance themselves or withdraw from family and friends, sometimes because they don't wish to be a burden or sometimes because they just need time to themselves. It is important as a carer not to take this personally and to try to be patient. Avoid making comments like 'cheer up' or 'you'll get over it'. Remember my analogy of getting stuck in the trough from Chapter 1? We don't have the capacity to just 'snap out of it'.

Consider offering help with day-to-day tasks.

These tasks may appear manageable normally, but for the person with mental health problems they may be overwhelming. I have shared examples of my difficulties with making decisions, concentration, low energy and motivation, and the impact of these on my ability to carry out simple tasks. During my journey I was dealing with loads of workers compensation reporting, and one of the ways my wife was able to support me was by taking on some of those responsibilities. She had problems with providing emotional support, but she found a way to help by keeping track of medical appointments, submitting certificates, managing payments and being the first point of contact for my case manager. I was grateful for that help because it freed me to focus on recovery.

One of the best things that family and friends can do in support is to take the time to *listen* to the person, setting aside any personal judgements that may arise. Listening to the person without pushing solutions can make them feel less alone and more understood. Displaying *empathy*, rather than sympathy, is the key. When they are withdrawn, gently check in with them from time to time. One of my most memorable sources of support was a mate, Steve, who had his own window manufacturing business. Steve generally had a sense of when I wasn't at my best, usually when he hadn't heard from me for a while, and out of the blue he would arrive at my house and knock on the door.

When I answered, he'd generally tell me he had a job in a nearby street and was just checking in to see if there was anything I needed. He never pressed me to invite him in, and he never stayed too long. Steve's visits were simple gestures that made me feel less alone and more understood, and they reminded me that I had people in my corner. To me, those thoughtful visits meant everything.

I strongly encourage those supporting loved ones to educate themselves. Consider undertaking a mental health first-aid course and/or a suicide prevention course. Learn how to have difficult conversations and be able to recognise warning signs of suicide and other crises. Supporting someone with mental health problems can be demanding, particularly during and after crises, so carers also need to take care of themselves. Self-care means dedicating time to doing things that lift your mood, refilling your emotional bucket. That might include some of the strategies I have shared in this book, including exercise, meditation and practising gratitude, or it could be a hobby or other interest. It might include the carer also seeking some professional support. Whatever it is that you find helpful to recharge, try to make time for it.

Offer encouragement during the person's recovery. Recognise accomplishments, effort and progress while avoiding criticism during tough times. Remember, the key ingredient for recovery is hope and belief, so try to nurture rather than stifle it. Sometimes it's one step back for every two steps forward, so hang in there while they are committing to their recovery treatments. Which brings me next to the inner ring.

Inner ring: Personal responsibility and commitment to action

My advice to those on a recovery journey

The lesson I learned on my own recovery journey that stood above all others is that mental health clinicians don't make people well again, and nor does medication. My clinicians didn't make me well again – they taught me strategies and guided me through therapy, but ultimately it was *me* who made me well again. The ultimate responsibility for recovery lies at the feet of the individual. Reaching recovery, whatever that may mean for you, involves lots of hard work and commitment, but it is totally worth it.

I know it's tough. I know there are days when you feel so worn down and broken that going on seems too hard. But just as many mental health problems have some origin in adverse life experiences, it is also life experiences that offer a way back. Educate yourself. A mechanic cannot fix a car before learning how it works. Read books or listen to podcasts to learn why you feel the way you do but also to find ways to start feeling better and develop a sense of hope and belief. Regain agency over your own recovery and remember that you are not your diagnoses – you are a person. You have a right to do your own research and to question treatment options suggested to you. You are the best expert on you.

As I mentioned earlier, what I have shared is *my* recovery journey, and what worked for me may not necessarily be the best fit for someone else. We are all different. We have different personalities, different upbringings, different belief systems, different abilities, different opportunities, different family and social networks and so much more. But there were 'inner ring' elements critical to my recovery that I believe apply broadly.

1. ***Commitment to professional help***

   Therapy was tough going at times, but to be effective it often needs to be. I think of it as short-term pain for long-term gain. Often our life experiences, including trauma, need to be properly processed before we can find acceptance, perhaps even forgiveness, so we can move on with a better life. Just as importantly, my clinicians taught me strategies that I would eventually put into practice to rewire my brain and live with my experiences much better.

2. ***Make a tailored recovery game plan***

   Before I made a plan, I was stuck in a negative victim mindset with no sense of direction and no hope for the future. Putting together a recovery game plan tailored to me and my challenges gave me a sense of hope and belief for the first time.

It allowed me to feel like I had some control over my situation. It gave me direction, with goals to work towards. It helped keep me motivated and on track. Sharing my game plan with those closest to me also gave them hope and a sense of what I needed regarding support. Most importantly, my recovery game plan kept me looking forward to a positive future rather than back at all that was lost.

3. ***Commit to action***

I stuck to my game plan, worked hard and committed to my recovery strategies. Setting small, achievable goals minimised the risk of surrender and gave me something to build on as I progressed. I was able to regularly tap into the satisfying feeling of reward as those goals were achieved, which encouraged motivation. Commitment to my game plan actions demonstrated responsibility not only to myself but to those closest to me as well. Keeping my actions flexible allowed me to increase the level of challenge when I was going well or to decrease it, without judgement, when I was not.

As far as the strategies I relied on for recovery went, although giving back through volunteer work had the biggest impact for me, I do not believe any one therapy I used in my game plan was responsible for my recovery. Cognitive behavioural therapy with those worksheets, for example, on its own would have contributed very little to my recovery outcomes. What it did, though, was provide me with a new skill for challenging my negative thinking to add to others in my recovery toolbox, all used in combination with each other and tailored to me.

4. ***Build social connections***

   Before having what I then called 'my mental breakdown', I had been an extremely social person with a massive network of friends. Afterwards, I lost contact with most of them and only maintained contact with a small number, preferring to keep to myself. My game plan actions provided opportunities to get out and meet people again. I have a tribal personality. I need a social network, a sense of community and a sense of *belonging*. My game plan, particularly with the work I was doing with those high-school kids, helped me get that back.

5. ***Learn new skills***

   Through my 'word art' mindfulness action I was developing new skills in descriptive writing, skills that would later bring life to my memoir. And I didn't realise it at the time but while I was delivering talks for the Black Dog Institute, I was developing new skills as an educator, facilitator and public speaker. I was learning how to engage with an audience and use body language, tone of voice and the power of a pause. I was learning how to *read* an audience and then how to fine-tune my message and delivery. Through listening to the experiences of others after presentations, I was broadening my mental health knowledge way past my own experience.

Learning these new skills exercised my brain, stimulated growth of new neural connections and pathways, and changed my brain structure for the better. Learning kept me motivated, engaged and striving for improvement, and it also filled me with self-belief. Learning something new is one of the best ways to enhance our sense of *worth*, and for me, learning all these new skills later opened doors to a new career I never dreamed of.

6. ***Give back***

   My work with the Black Dog Institute was done as a volunteer. I was blissfully unaware that I was benefiting from the deep healing power of giving back for the benefit of others for no financial reward.

7. ***Turn negatives to positives***

   I turned what I had seen as a negative experience into a positive one and all those years of loss into something worth living through. In using my experience to help others, I turned my mental health adversity into an *advantage*. Rather than staying stuck in a negative victim mindset, I chose to 'reframe' the way I looked at my situation, embracing the more positive mindset of being in control.

8. *Have a purpose*

During my police career I had an amazing sense of purpose, but when it ended so suddenly, I had none. For those three years I felt worthless. But working as a volunteer for the Black Dog Institute gave me a new sense of purpose and lifted my self-esteem. When people asked me what I was doing with myself, I could proudly answer, 'I'm working with the Black Dog Institute, teaching kids about mental health', and to that I'd generally receive positive words of thanks and encouragement.

Often people think the primary reason they get up and go to work every day is to pay the bills, cover the mortgage, pay school fees and so on, which is true to a point. But we rarely reflect on the benefits of work in terms of our wellbeing. This may be an overgeneralisation, but for me, the biggest benefit I receive from going to work, both paid and unpaid, is the sense of purpose it gives. We often don't realise how much we need that sense of purpose until we find ourselves out of work for whatever reason.

Through volunteer work I built a new identity

that helped replace the one I lost. I now knew myself as Craig Semple, mental health advocate and educator, and others were getting to know me as this too. My grief for a lost police career and identity was finally resolved.

9. ***Embrace challenge***
   Staying safe in our comfort zone may provide a sense of security, but it also ensures we stay exactly the same. The path to personal growth comes only from stepping out of our comfort zone towards things that challenge us in a safe way. Personal growth happened for me by gradually increasing the level of challenge with each of the small, achievable actions on my game plan over time. The more I made progress, the more I increased the challenge and, from that, the more I made progress. Personal growth happened from safely stepping out of my comfort zone, making myself vulnerable, and sharing my personal story publicly. Terrified at first, the more talks I delivered, the more confident I became and the stronger I grew. Rather than *going* through recovery, I was *growing* through recovery. By constantly lifting the bar a little higher, by challenging myself, I was no longer surviving. I was *thriving*.

The core: Hope and belief

The *inner ring* of personal responsibility and commitment to action is where recovery outcomes are made possible while being supported by the *outer ring* of professional help and love from family and friends. But it is what lies at the *core* of the rings of recovery that provides the motivation, the commitment, the willpower and a beacon of light for direction.

The core is *hope* and *belief*. Find it. Nourish it. Build on it.

I have shared my recovery journey, and yours is there for the taking. Learn some strategies, make a plan and believe, because not only is it possible to recover from mental health problems, it is also possible to come out the other side even stronger.

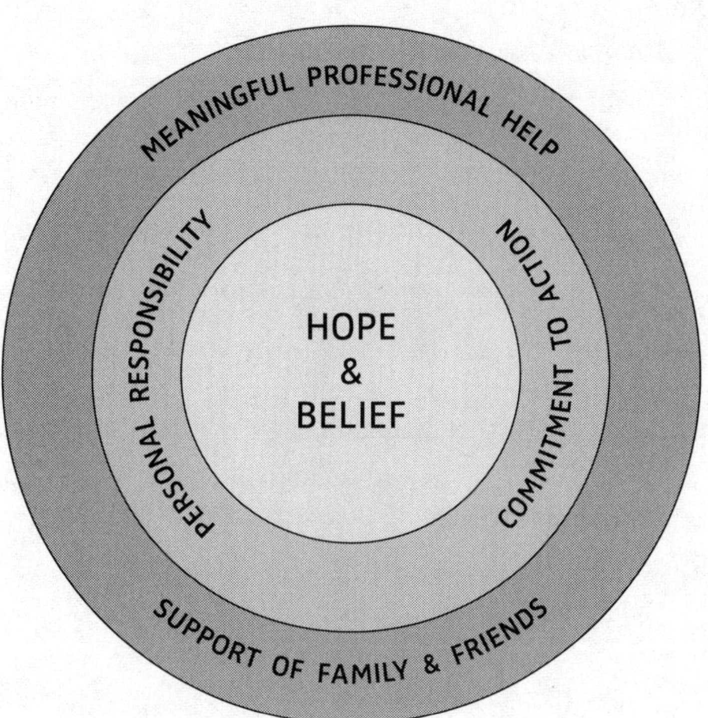
MEANINGFUL PROFESSIONAL HELP
PERSONAL RESPONSIBILITY
COMMITMENT TO ACTION
HOPE
&
BELIEF
SUPPORT OF FAMILY & FRIENDS

PART 3

POST-TRAUMATIC GROWTH

CHAPTER 15

Building on recovery

My year of big challenges was 2017, the year when I really tested the boundaries of my recovery. The first big challenge commenced the year before.

In 2016, a great friend, PTSD survivor and former police colleague, Leeann Lloyd, came along to a talk I delivered to teachers and parents at a private school near Grafton. In the audience that evening was the husband of a teacher, Scott, who was a former New South Wales prison officer and a volunteer rural fire service captain. Scott had his own story of living with PTSD, and afterwards he introduced himself to Leeann and me. He told us he was in the process of buying a business he had been working for that led treks through Papua New Guinea, including the legendary Kokoda Track. Every year, Kokoda Campaign Tours chose a charity to support through their treks, and after listening to me, he offered to support the

Black Dog Institute in 2017.

Leeann looked at me and said, 'You realise if you are on board with this then you and I are going on one of the treks next year, don't you?'

'No way on earth am I doing that, Leeann!' I adamantly replied.

And that's how on 11 April 2017, I found myself stepping out of a small plane on an airfield in the middle of the Papuan jungle.

Scott and Leeann had worked hard on me, and the fact they were doing this to help financially support the volunteer work I was doing made it hard to say no. My biggest reservation was whether I was mentally up to the challenge. I was confident of my physical capabilities, but I was acutely aware that trekking more than a hundred kilometres up and down massive mountains through dense jungle, being cut off from the outside world and living in tents with a small group of people for ten days was going to be even more of a mental challenge than physical. I guess I had found a new comfort zone with my mental health, and I was a little worried that this trek may be pushing things along too quickly. I just wasn't sure I was up to it, and that fear of failure had been reinforced looking out from my window on that small plane.

We had flown from Port Moresby to Kokoda, directly over the impenetrable jungle we had to trek back through, and as I watched mountain range after soaring mountain range disappear beneath our aeroplane, with every horizon more of the same as far as my eyes could see, I just couldn't fathom our return journey could possibly be done on foot. I kept reminding myself that these guys had done this many times and knew what they were doing. As it turned out, they did know what they were doing, and not only did I safely complete the trek but I had some profound experiences along the way.

Never in my life have I been so moved at a deeply emotional level by the environment around me. Every steep mountain range we climbed rewarded me with the most spectacular views, and then slipping and sliding down rock faces and mud on the other side rewarded me with rivers of roaring white-water rapids and waterfalls. The incredible beauty of many of the places we passed through is difficult to describe, because in the moment it was magnified exponentially by the sense of reward from the effort of getting there. Practising mindfulness and meditation allowed me to completely immerse myself and appreciate the world around me. Crossing one ravine, I was so struck by what I saw that I let everyone else walk ahead. I sat on a boulder for a while on my own, taking in the damp, earthy scents and the cool air on my wet skin while enjoying a waterfall cascading through pockets of tropical plants and colourful flowers so well placed that the picture could never be replicated by design. I sat and let it all penetrate me, absorbing it to the point where, unashamedly, tears flowed freely down my face.

In that one moment, I knew beyond doubt that after many, many years of emotional numbness, I could truly, deeply *feel* again.

So many of my experiences on that trek provide parallel lessons with mental health recovery. When we fell, there was always a hand ready to help us up. If someone was struggling, someone else would step in and carry their pack until they recovered. During the most difficult times, there was always a person who could turn the whole arduous experience into something funny, and we would get through it with laughter. It was a lesson in the importance of good, reliable *support*, not only of offering it but also of accepting it.

Another parallel was the importance of social connections and having a sense of community. I had travelled through parts of developing countries, including West Timor and South Sumatra, in previous years on surfing trips and never failed to be fascinated by the ability of people with so little to be so happy. My experience with the people of Papua New Guinea was no different. Obviously poverty brings with it plenty of misery, but so can excess and wealth, and one thing people in these countries do way better than those of us in wealthy developed nations is *community*. Huts are not locked, kids roam free, everybody knows everybody, and there is no preoccupation with ownership of material possessions. Our decline in collective community spirit and belonging is no doubt contributing to a corresponding decline in mental and emotional wellbeing. Social connection is an important element for wellbeing and mental health recovery, as is one final and important parallel lesson.

Looking at the *big picture* from the aeroplane on that first day had made the whole objective look so unachievable and out of reach. Once on the ground, though, rather than being overwhelmed by the magnitude of the overall challenge, I broke it all down into small, achievable goals like 'just get to the top of the next ridge', focusing simply on putting one foot in front of the other and achieving the goal one step at a time. Just like recovery. And one step at a time, one small goal after another, we all made it to the finish.

▪ ▪ ▪

Soon after my return from Kokoda, I was invited to join a new program being developed to support former police officers and their families. Backup for Life (B4L) was being funded by the state government and administered by the New South Wales Police Legacy charity. The program was managed by a fully paid co-ordinator and assistant, with the other roles, including mine, performed by volunteers.

There were about ten of us, all former police officers, who originally joined the program as mentors, all trained and available to offer support and advice to other former police and families, many of whom were in crisis from PTSD, depression, alcohol addiction, relationship breakdowns, financial crisis and much more. I was still working as a volunteer speaker for the Black Dog Institute, but this new role was a whole new challenge for me. Over the first twelve months we dedicated most of our time to building and promoting the program, but as word spread, I started meeting up with an increasing number of former cops at cafés, parks, their homes and other places. Some just needed to be heard by someone who understood, someone who had lived with what they were living with. Some were in crisis, just before or after suicide attempts. I attended appointments with some and supported them through meetings with lawyers and other professionals. Mostly, though, I simply listened.

I had already received a real education through my own journey, but having this exposure to the journeys of others served to build on that experience, broadening my awareness and understanding of illness and recovery challenges. I was not there to offer clinical advice or to be a counsellor. I was there to listen, support and guide them towards services that could help. Above all else, though, I discovered over time that the most valuable thing I could offer was hope. Knowing where I had been, they could see how far I'd come, 'and if Craig got through it, I can get through it too'. Hope and belief – the key elements that make recovery possible.

Between working for Black Dog and Backup for Life, I was now almost full-time volunteering, and I loved it. My role with B4L provided me with a real sense of returning to the police family I had missed so much, of making new friends, of *belonging*. I rapidly built on my recovery to become more rounded and well-adjusted than I had been at any other time in my life. That doesn't mean life was suddenly all lollipops and unicorns; I still had my ups and downs, but I really felt that I had so much more self-awareness and was able to manage life better. Well enough, in fact, to consider working again.

During my first year with Backup for Life, our co-ordinator, Cath, led us all through the Mental Health First Aid course as an accredited instructor. The two days of training provided in-depth education on how to support people experiencing common mental illnesses and how to help with crises, including suicide. I had never heard of this training before, but having sat through it, I was impressed with the content. At the conclusion of the course, Cath pulled me aside and asked me if I would be interested in becoming an instructor.

'Craig, you are already educating people. You have the skills to deliver this. You could be trained as an instructor, start your own business and deliver this course through it.'

For the five years since my medical retirement, I had never believed there was anything I was qualified to do other than law enforcement. Being a cop was all I knew, but that door was closed to me. I had never considered the wealth of transferable skills I had accrued over my police experience, but now Cath planted a seed of thought. Not once as a volunteer did I consider using that experience professionally in a new career. I couldn't imagine charging a fee for something I loved doing so much as a volunteer, but I was no longer on workers compensation, and I had a family to provide for. So, with a mighty leap of faith, in October 2017 I founded Mentality Plus Pty Limited.

■ ■ ■

For the first few months I laid the groundwork, developing a website and products. I found a fabulous accountant who became my business advisor, taking care of the structural and financial processes. I travelled to Brisbane and completed the Mental Health First Aid instructor's course. I fine-tuned my lived-experience talk for delivery in workplaces and conference events and started an informal partnership with a registered training organisation in Newcastle. When I told my mate Shannon at the Black Dog Institute about my new business, she immediately had me approved to deliver paid talks to BDI workplace clients.

Everything looked promising, but in all honesty, my levels of stress and worry seemed to increase with each passing month. Bookings were few and intermittent, and I had a palpable fear of failure that if this didn't work out, I had placed my family in a difficult financial position. I gave a lot of thought to how I could reduce this fear, and eventually I realised that I needed a *backup plan*. I had learned the importance of having a backup plan the hard way. I didn't have one during my police career because I didn't believe I'd ever need it, so I had nothing to fall back on when I did. I often discuss the importance of having a backup plan during resilience programs, and I have found most people don't have one. A backup plan doesn't need to be complicated; it just needs to be enough to catch us if we fall. For my backup plan, I decided to harness the knowledge and experience from my career as a detective. I put Mentality Plus aside for a while (my plan A) and got to work obtaining the qualifications and licences needed to work as a private investigator. It took a while, and I hoped I'd never have to do investigative work again, but it was worth it. I now had a backup plan, my plan B, which reduced the stress caused by fear of failure and provided me with a sense of security. I had something to catch me if I fell.

The main reason bookings were low and building momentum was difficult was my geographical isolation. I lived in a small community north of Coffs Harbour, a tourist region full of small businesses but lacking significant industry or potential clients. The limited work I did secure involved extensive travel, mainly to Newcastle and other places, which added cost to clients, and at that time I was probably running at about fifteen percent of my potential booking capacity. My wife had a secure job and I still had one son in high school, so I could see no way around this difficulty until 2018, when life threw me another big challenge and I arrived at a significant turning point in my life.

Although this book is not about my family life, earlier I shared a little of the difficulties with my marriage. I mentioned that soon after I made my recovery game plan in 2015, my wife and I reconciled, and I was invited back into our family home. But relationships are complicated. Sometimes I struggle to find the words to adequately describe the last few years of my marriage even to myself, let alone others. There was so much damage and trauma in our marriage, in my family and in her family, that I don't know how I expected it to work. But I did go back to her, and we did try again. Two years later I found myself out of home, again not by choice, and again I found myself looking for somewhere to live, all while trying to start a business. Then, at the point where I had made a new plan and was ready to move on, I was asked back a second time.

So many people have asked me since, why would you do that to yourself? Why would I keep going back to a situation that was hopeless and threatened all the hard work I committed to getting my health back on track? The answers were simple, really. First, I felt like I *owed* it to my wife and my family for everything they had put up with during my police career. Second, I didn't want to give up on my family and my kids. Third, I kept hoping that things would change. But then, in July 2018, it all happened again, the third time in four years. The two previous separations had both nearly broken me; this time, though, I was better prepared. This time I decided that whatever I felt I owed had been paid back in full, and what I did next taught me another important lesson in navigating tough times.

It was the power of taking advantage of the *opportunities* presented during life's challenges and adversities.

▪▪▪

I had arrived at a fork in the road. One path was to find a rental close to my family home so I could be near my sixteen- and nineteen-year-old sons and make life as good as I could. But with a struggling business, I would eventually burn through my financial resources. The other path involved throwing everything in on a big risk. It involved moving further away, possibly interstate, to somewhere I could re-establish my business and give it the best chance of success.

I considered all my potential business locations, including capital cities, but I kept coming back to my old home town of the Hunter Region. Newcastle is the seventh largest city in Australia by population, it supports a massive resource industry, it has a large airport providing access right across Australia and it is only two hours from all the business opportunities of

Sydney. It was also home to the training company I had a relationship with. And even more importantly than the business opportunities, Newcastle had something else I desperately needed: a solid group of lifelong friends from high school. So right in the middle of one big emotional challenge in my life, I pushed it to the edge by taking on another one and moved five hours away to another city.

I love the water, so I secured a very small, cheap, two-bedroom flat, sight unseen, in a unit complex at Swan Bay in Lake Macquarie. I put a spare bed, a few sticks of old furniture and the TV from my man cave on a removalist truck. I hooked up a trailer loaded with my motorbike and a few bits and pieces and hit the highway south, back to my place of birth. Back home.

Walking through the door of my rented flat for the first time, I was totally unprepared for the experience. I passed through the empty rooms of the old, worn-out unit, taking in the state of disrepair, then landed back in the tiny living room and dropped to the floor, where I cried long and hard. At some point I settled down, leaned back against a cold brick wall and thought about things. I was shocked at my reaction and reflected on the reasons why being here had hit me so hard. One was that I was understandably upset about the end of my marriage and all the emotional baggage that went with it, but that wasn't something I could fix straight away. That was part of a grieving process and would take time. The other reason, though, one that I could fix immediately, was that I felt like a complete failure.

For twenty-three years, my wife and I always had our own home wherever we moved, and over those years we worked extremely hard to finally pay out the mortgage. Our last home, the one I left, was a large and expensive house on ten acres of elevated rainforest with beautiful ocean views. Walking into this tiny, run-down, rented flat after what I had was like being physically hit with a realisation: 'Look how far you've fallen. Look what your life has become.' I carefully considered this while sitting on the hard lino floor and started feeling a little ashamed of myself for allowing an attitude of self-pity to set in.

'Mate, if this is how you react to where you now find yourself then you *needed* this to happen,' I said out loud to the empty room.

Like many, my beginnings were modest, but I had grown too comfortable in the life of privilege I had built for myself and my family, and I had been taking what I had for granted. With those words spoken out loud, I made up my mind that this experience was going to be *good* for me, not bad. That this was an opportunity to reset and start again. It was an opportunity to readjust the living standards I had become comfortable with and simplify my life with less. Once again, I intended to turn a negative into a positive and loss into gain, and with that, I got off the floor and set about making this run-down flat my *home*.

So the first opportunity I seized from the challenge

of my separation and move to Newcastle was to use it to strengthen my resilience. The second opportunity was to kickstart Mentality Plus.

■ ■ ■

About the same time as my move, I delivered my first professional presentation as a keynote speaker to an audience of five hundred at an emergency services conference in Sydney, and that conference was like a starting gun being fired.

Now I was firmly established in the Newcastle area, the training company I was affiliated with got serious about promoting me to local clients, and once I got in front of a few, my bookings increased. Since I was closer to Sydney, my workplace bookings with the Black Dog Institute increased, and I also started training and evaluating other retired cops to become mentors for the Backup for Life program. Suddenly, I was quite busy. Within two or three months of moving to Newcastle, I had taken my business from about fifteen percent of booking capacity to closer to eighty percent.

Then my friend Shannon Nolan left the Black Dog Institute to take a position with Virgin Australia Airlines, and she took me with her. After running one program for the senior executives, I found myself travelling all over Australia for an entire year delivering mental health training to four hundred managers and care crew. Now I was flat out, fully booked to a hundred percent capacity, and it didn't stop there. If there is one lesson I have learned from starting and building a business, momentum is everything, and by the end of the second year after moving to Newcastle, I could proudly say I was the director of a very successful company.

I have learned through the many challenges I have faced in my life that some of the most profound and life-changing adversities can also offer the most profound and life-changing *opportunities* if we are prepared to look for them. Like gratitude, being able to take some *advantage* from an adversity makes it a little less adverse. Does the fact that my separation and subsequent divorce led to the opportunity for me to achieve business success make my divorce worth going through? No way, but it did make the whole experience less painful and reduced my sense of loss.

Looking for opportunities during tough times has become one of my key strategies of looking forward to a positive future rather than looking back at all that is lost.

CHAPTER 16

Growing through adversity

In Chapter 14 I discussed that for me, resilience means facing adversity and putting strategies in place to overcome it, with those strategies becoming the learned behaviours I fall back on when I face other adversities in my life. In February 2020, I had an opportunity to put that whole theory to the test.

As word of a new disease spreading across the world started to sink in here in Australia, I had already braced myself for the impending impact on my business and livelihood. When my first booking was cancelled by a client in January, it was clear to me where this was all headed. That cancellation was soon followed by another, and then another, until they were all cancelled by early February. I sat in front of the television every day watching everything I had worked so long and hard to build being torn down in a matter of days and weeks. My future income evaporated before my eyes and I felt powerless to do anything about it, and to compound the loss, my divorce settlement finalised around the same time, so then I was dealing with two massive financial losses at once. My plans of taking out a mortgage and buying my own home were indefinitely put on hold as I now needed the deposit to live on. Future income lost, past income being used to survive. It didn't look good.

As bad as it was, I really did try to stay as positive as possible, but in doing so I was suppressing everything I was truly feeling, so the positivity was only skin-deep. I have learned from my mental health journey and lots of therapy that when I try to push down negative emotions, they tend to start escaping sideways into my relationships, sleep, levels of stress and emotional wellbeing. One morning I rose, made a pot of tea, sat down in front of the television and started watching more Covid catastrophes being played out on the news. The longer I watched, the more anger I could feel welling up inside me. At some point, while trying to push it down and not let it get to me, I stopped and thought to myself, *Mate, stop trying to pretend you're not angry. You have every right to be angry. Who wouldn't be? Admit it. Allow it to happen. Allow yourself to be completely pissed off.*

And that's what I decided to do, but I also put controls around it. First, my anger was not allowed to adversely affect other people. Second, I gave myself permission to be really pissed off and let it all out, but only for that day. I could be angry for that day and then the next, I would sit down and work on a plan to survive the crisis.

So all that day, I stomped around with a really bad attitude. I walked into the gym mid-morning, before the lockdowns had begun, and was greeted warmly as always by the manager.

'Hey, Craig. How are you today?'

In place of my usual cheerful reply, she got hit with, 'I'm actually really pissed off today, Judie. But don't worry, it's only for today. I'll be all good tomorrow.' And then I walked off to my workout leaving her a little bemused.

All that day I allowed myself to be angry, and wow, it felt good. It was such a *release*. And when I woke the next morning, incredibly, all that anger was gone. I felt none of it. I had allowed it, processed it, and I was ready to confront my situation with clarity using the rational, analytical part of my brain.

▪▪▪

The starting point of my recovery from severe mental illness was my game plan. During each of my marital separations, I sat down and wrote out a game plan. Game-planning my way through adversities had become an embedded life skill that I now fell back on to help survive a global pandemic.

Divide and conquer

During many years of psychological therapy, I was regularly reminded to focus on the things I had control over rather than the things I didn't. I later saw a leadership presentation where this very simple concept was brilliantly modelled as something developed by author Stephen Covey as circles of concern, influence and control. The method I used was a little more rudimentary but had served me well during past challenges.

The morning after 'rage day', I sat down with a pen and paper and wrote a list of everything in my life that was causing me worry, and I mean *everything*. Once I had that list, and it was quite long, I went through a process I call *divide and conquer*. I went through every challenge on my list and, being objective, put a line through the ones that I had little or no control over. I was ruthless in this, and I needed to be. There was no point wasting emotional time and energy worrying about the challenges that were outside my control, like *what if the pandemic drags on for a long time*, or *this is causing me massive financial loss*, or *all my business momentum has been lost*. These were things I had been ruminating on, but they were also things I couldn't control, so I put a line through them. The concerns that remained were things that I felt I could 'do' something about, like *what am I going to do to adapt my business?* I made a list of all the concerns that I had some control over and then wrote down ideas of *how* I could influence each of them. This first step in my game plan, the strategy of divide and conquer, allowed me to clearly identify key challenges and actions to consider in overcoming them.

During times of adversity and challenge, we often become overwhelmed and unable to see a way through. Negative thoughts of looming catastrophe, self-criticism, hopelessness, blame or failure create a positive feedback loop, completely blocking rational thinking processes. Often, when we drill down on our worries, we will find that many of our concerns are about things that are either partially or completely out of our control. An effective method for reducing feelings of overwhelm is to divide our concerns into two clearly defined categories (or three in Covey's model):

- the concerns we have no control over
- the concerns that are within our control and influence.

Then we can concentrate our focus and energy on the concerns we can do something about rather than those we can't.

A last example. One morning during the early months of the pandemic, when I was sitting in front of the television every morning watching news coverage, my twenty-two-year-old son, Owen, who was living with me at the time, walked from his bedroom and to the kitchen, looked at the TV then at me, and asked,

'What are you watching that shit for, Dad?'

'Because I have a business and I need to know what's going on!' I rebuffed.

'Yeah, but look what it's doing to you.'

Owen and I have very different personalities and world views and have often locked horns over them, but this time I was left speechless. I had no response because he was right. I sat and looked at the television screen through new eyes, no longer seeing important news and information. What I saw behind the program hosts was a blood-red graphic with ugly animated viruses floating around, a list of infection rates and fatalities and other nasty statistics running down one side. What I saw was mainstream media instilling fear, because fear is addictive, and fear keeps you coming back because you're scared. When I thought about it, my continual exposure to this negative fearmongering was making me more stressed, more irritable and a little depressed. Owen was right.

I had no control over how mainstream media was covering the pandemic, but I did have control over my exposure to it. From that day, I stopped watching the morning programs and most mainstream news. I still needed information for my business, so for that I checked the daily updates and briefings on government websites. I was getting all the information I needed without the emotional hype thrown in. Then I turned my attention to my social media accounts, and as much as I have never been very active on them, the pandemic had spawned a wave of negativity and vitriol that I was better off without. After turning off my television, I said goodbye in a post on my Facebook account and promptly deactivated it. It stayed deactivated for three years, and it was great.

I have always liked watching the news and reading newspapers with a coffee, and I still do, but from time to time I will place a self-imposed media embargo for a few weeks when I feel it is starting to get to me. Big tech, social media and mainstream media goliaths have way too much control over our lives, but we have the power to take it back. We have choice.

Strengths and vulnerabilities

Once I had a list of the challenges, I had control over deciding the actions and goals that would hopefully see me coming through the pandemic in the best shape possible. The first stage of setting goals was writing a list of my strengths and vulnerabilities.

I first turned my attention to my weaknesses and considered the shortcomings that might leave me vulnerable through the pandemic. Identifying my vulnerabilities helped with my game plan in the following ways:

- It allowed me to identify the shortcomings in my life, personality, behaviours and skills that may reduce my chances of achieving set goals.
- It helped me assess which weaknesses could be

easily strengthened so I didn't waste time focusing on those that may be too difficult to address.

- It helped me consider what external support I'd need.

Having dealt with the negatives, I finished on a positive by writing a list of all the strengths I possessed that would help me through the crisis. Identifying my strengths was a critical part of my Covid game-planning in the following ways:

- Attaining set goals was far more achievable if those goals aligned with my strengths.
- Listing my strengths helped me focus on the good things about my character, personality and life. It served to lift my self-esteem and built a sense of confidence and control. It gave me a sense of 'I can do this'.

Identifying some of my obvious strengths was a relatively easy task, but others were not so obvious. To help with this, I thought of the positive things I have been commended for, such as in feedback from clients, and the qualities that have helped me through past challenges. I considered the skills and experience I had acquired over my life. By the time I finished with my strengths, I was saying to myself, *Mate, compared to the other adversities you have faced in your life, this is nothing. If you survived all those, you will survive this as well.*

When I had my lists, next to each vulnerability I wrote down what I could do to strengthen it, and for my strengths I wrote down how I could harness it. For example, a strength I identified from client feedback is that I had a powerful physical presence in front of an audience. I could no longer stand in front of audiences, but the next best thing would be to record videos of my talks and workshops and make them available to clients via subscription. This became a short-term goal. A vulnerability I identified was that when it comes to tech and IT, I am a dinosaur, so to strengthen that vulnerability I decided to outsource what I could and get help and training to manage everything else. This also became a short-term goal. Which brings me to the next step in game-planning: setting goals.

Setting goals

The success of my mental health recovery game plan five years earlier was in large part because I set small, achievable goals that minimised the risk of surrender and gave me something to build on while I worked towards the ultimate goal of regaining my mental health. I applied the same principle to the goals I set to survive the pandemic, setting short-term goals and endgame goals.

My *short-term goals* were bite-sized ones that I could achieve along the way. Setting and accomplishing small short-term goals helped me enjoy a motivating sense of reward through achievement while working towards my long-term goals. Aligning my goals with my strengths made them more achievable, so one of my short-term goals was to record my talks and workshops. I was introduced to Michael, a local self-employed commercial and video producer who, like me, had also had all his work cancelled. Over the next few months, I met Michael at various locations to capture my talks on video. It was a full commercial enterprise, with multiple cameras, green screen and lighting, and it took a few months because, in all honesty, I was completely hopeless at it. In front of a live audience I had interaction, I had feedback through body language, I had *connection*. In front of a camera I had nothing, just a cold, black, shiny lens. Eventually we managed to get it all recorded, but in the end I never used them, not once. Does the fact that I have never used those recordings make all those hours of work over several months a waste of time? Absolutely not! It was a great investment in time because working on those recordings challenged me, kept me motivated, kept me looking forward to the future and gave me a sense of purpose. Working on those recordings allowed me to build new skills in speaking to a camera, which was invaluable by the time I started delivering talks through communications platforms like Teams and Zoom.

My *endgame goals* were long-term targets about where I aimed to be when the pandemic ended. One of those was simply to come out of this crisis in a stronger position than I was in before it. It was a lofty goal, but it was achievable, and it kept me working hard, fostered creativity and gave me hope for an even better future for Mentality Plus.

One of the best ways to overcome feelings of helplessness and victimhood during times of adversity is to set goals. Setting goals in challenging times will help to:

- provide hope for the future
- avoid being trapped in a negative victim mindset
- narrow focus towards positive actions
- motivate
- provide the pleasure of reward as goals are achieved
- maximise chances of achieving desired outcomes.

In the beginning, like everyone, I had no idea how long the pandemic would last or when business would be back to normal, but I did know that there would be an end to it eventually. My endgame goal was that when it was over and the starting gun fired, I aimed to be ready not *at* the starting line but to already have one foot *over* it. To achieve that mighty goal, I fell back on my favourite strategy of *looking for opportunities*.

Opportunities

Like I said earlier, some of the most profound, life-changing adversities often provide the most profound, life-changing *opportunities*. The pandemic, with all the loss of life, loss of freedom, loss of livelihoods and associated misery, was no exception. For me, the biggest opportunity the pandemic offered was *time*.

Over the previous couple of years, I'd had so many ideas about workshop development and new products, but while travelling the country delivering existing programs, I was too busy to work on them. Now I had time. Since my medical retirement from the police force I had written a memoir, starting it as a form of therapy and later seeing its potential as a book. Just before my separation I had sent the draft manuscript to professional editors, and although the feedback was great, if I wanted it published it needed an enormous amount of work. For the next couple of years I was so busy that I had no opportunity to work on it, so it sat as an untouched file on my hard drive, going nowhere. But now I had time.

These opportunities and others helped set up my backup plan, my plan B if plan A took a hit, and once I had my backup plan, my pandemic game plan was complete. I sat back, proud of my plan, full of hope and optimism, and then remembered one last strategy: giving back.

Although I had been busy professionally, I had still dedicated hundreds of hours every year to giving back by volunteering with Backup for Life and at other community mental health events. Giving back remained one of my key wellbeing strategies, but now everything was shut down, even volunteering opportunities were limited. Then I thought about all the other small business owners who were in the same position as me and wondered how many of them had the time or knowledge to put together a plan. From that, I had an idea to develop a structured game-planning workbook, using examples from my own business game plan, in the hope that it might help others. I started on it straight away. It took a couple of weeks, but when finished I had a forty-four-page workbook ready to go, complete with strategy worksheets and illustrations. I called it *Growing Through Covid*, put out an invitation on social media (this being a few weeks before I deactivated it) and sent it out for free to whoever wanted a copy to work with. Giving back through sharing knowledge and experience gave me a keen sense of purpose and self-worth, and it provided a gateway to networking with other small businesses that, at a time of significant isolation, was priceless.

Scaffolding

I had a practical, hands-on game plan in place to get me and my business through the pandemic, but as robust as that plan was, I was also aware the journey would be filled with stressful challenges. To manage that I made a wellbeing plan that I called *scaffolding*.

After my mental health recovery, I continued with the strategies I used to get well, and my recovery game plan became my wellbeing game plan. Covid lockdowns caused disruption to some of my main strategies, especially exercise, so I decided to draw up a revised wellbeing plan to maximise my mental, emotional and physical health throughout the many stressful challenges of the pandemic. The Cambridge Dictionary defines scaffolding as a structure designed to support, bolster, cradle, shore up, brace, prop and underpin, and all of those things are what my wellbeing plan did for me. A renewed commitment to adapted exercise and meditation practices kept my stress levels manageable during one of the toughest challenges of my life, reducing negative impacts on my physical and mental health, which helped me get through.

For every significant challenge I face or at times of high demands with stress, I renew my commitment to lifestyle adjustments that scaffold my wellbeing.

■ ■ ■

For me, like millions of others across the country and the world, Covid brought its fair share of loss. I lost opportunities to visit people I loved and to say proper goodbyes to some who passed, and my financial losses were colossal. But my Covid game plan not only saved my business, it also provided the platform to bounce back stronger than ever. When that starting gun fired, I was already two steps down the track.

The feedback I received from my *Growing Through Covid* workbooks was so positive that I realised there was an opportunity to adapt the concepts into a workplace resilience program. Covid was a challenge that we all experienced together, so the pandemic was a useful example to demonstrate strategies that can help when other adversities challenge us in life. *Growing Through Adversity* is now a popular program that would never have happened if not for Covid.

Once that program was embedded, I developed another program to help prepare police officers leaving the force through medical retirement, particularly those with psychological injuries. Three pilot *Growing Through Transition* programs were funded by EML insurance in 2022, and on the back of incredible feedback from those who attended, the programs are now a permanent offering to transitioning police officers and fully supported by the New South Wales Police Force. Through sharing what I have learned in my own recovery and successful transition and drawing on the countless experiences of those I have supported, these programs offer what these officers need most: a little hope and belief, and an awareness that they are not alone. Once again, this opportunity would not have occurred if it wasn't for the adversity of Covid.

By having a game plan to navigate this adversity, I not only survived it but even achieved my endgame goal of coming out the other side even stronger. Rather than *going through* the adversity, I was *growing through* it, and I'll come back to this in the final chapter.

But there was one more opportunity that I seized from the challenge of Covid. I took the opportunity of time offered to me during the pandemic to rewrite and complete my first book, *The Cop Who Fell to Earth*, which was published in August 2023. This, one of my life's proudest achievements, would not have happened if not for one of my life's toughest challenges. Nor would the book you are reading now have come about, which leads me to my final recovery strategy and one I touched on earlier in the mindfulness chapter: journaling.

CHAPTER 17

Journaling

My first experience of using writing as therapy came quite by accident. During my medical retirement from the police force in 2012, I was asked by my treating doctor for a short chronology of all the events that I believed contributed to my psychological injury. Eight months later I printed a sixty-page document and delivered it to him. It was sixty pages of all the horrors and traumas that I could recall from twenty-five years of policing. Just the ones I could remember.

Dr Kramer was a little surprised by the size of the document, normally receiving a dot-point list of incidents including date, where it occurred and brief details. But when I started writing my chronology, I immediately sensed a benefit to exploring and describing each of those events in much more detail than was expected. Although it was difficult to relive past traumatic experiences, it was also cathartic. It gave me a chance to understand and reflect on *why* it was that I was so unwell. I was *confronting* those events rather than running from them, which helped begin the healing process.

After delivering the chronology to my doctor, I decided to go home and start all over again, this time writing about my entire life, from childhood right through to the end of my career, and not just the bad events but the good, the funny, the incredible and the exciting events as well. I intended to record it while everything was still fresh in my memory so that one day my sons could read it and understand what I did. I wanted them to one day be proud of me. I wanted to write it all down, pack it up and put it all behind me so I could move forward with my life.

And so that's what I did. I bought a new laptop and got started early in 2013, but it didn't happen all at once. There were long periods where I was so unwell or in various stages of treatment that I had to stop, and sometimes I would go nowhere near it for months. But during the times I was able to write, I enjoyed it. I enjoyed reminiscing on old times, old friends, fun, laughter. It was tough writing about some of my experiences, especially those involving significant hurt, both committed and received, and those involving trauma, but after fully exploring those experiences through the writing process, once each was finished I was able to pack it away and move on. And the negative experiences were counterbalanced when writing about the good things over my life and all my achievements. It was a kind of exposure therapy, I guess. When I was writing I felt as though I had purpose, and I was also able to enjoy a sense of achievement after concluding a period of my life. Writing or *journaling* was a game plan strategy I committed to for my entire recovery journey and beyond. It took five long years to complete, but the process of recording those first forty-seven years of my life in written words gave my police career, my *life*, true meaning.

As I mentioned earlier, once finished I had sent the full manuscript to professional editors who returned it with assessment reports that, although positive, gave me pause for further reflection. First, because I literally wrote down everything significant, it was way too long, over three hundred thousand words, and a publisher would look at no more than one hundred thousand. Second, the objective critical assessments highlighted language and attitudes that to others would be questionable, and I think this especially highlights the benefits of journaling. When I now read back over my original memoir, I can see how my language has changed over time from maverick, reckless and sometimes judgemental in early writing to more reflective and circumspect later on. Writing provided the opportunity to question my own attitudes and beliefs and then make choices about those that did not reflect the type of person I aimed to be.

Writing was, and still is, one of my favoured approaches to processing my thoughts and life experiences. When I commit to writing about my experiences, both bad and good, it requires me to prise the experience apart, teasing out my beliefs and opinions and feelings at a depth that talking about them cannot reach. It is not just the writing that works for me but the reading back as well. I often write about an experience or opinion, thinking that I have it accurately articulated, then I read back over it and think, 'No, I don't think that's quite correct', which promotes further reflection. I'll tease it out and write it again until I'm fully satisfied that it is as accurate as words can reflect. For me, writing is a form of *mindfulness*. Rather than having thoughts and memories bouncing around in my head, writing allows me to focus on them one at a time, and with order rather than chaos.

Many psychologists encourage clients to write about life events, particularly those involving trauma or hurt, as a way of processing those experiences. This could be in the form of an unsent letter to oneself or to someone else who has inflicted physical, emotional or psychological injury. There are many programs available to help people tell their stories and express their experiences, a great example being the Australian Writers' Centre's 'Personal Storytelling for Veterans and First Responders'. Current and former military veterans and emergency service first responders can participate in a six-week course aimed at providing an outlet for expression, healing and creativity while being taught writing and communication skills that can be used in other careers.

Writing about traumatic life experiences can be a very cathartic process, but for people considering it, make sure you have support. Because writing often provokes deep reflection on experiences, it can also bring to the surface strong feelings and emotions. During the writing of this book, for example, I have reflected on experiences not previously explored, which I needed a little help unpacking. Writing about some of the experiences I have previously explored, like the crisis involving my dad, brought back feelings strong enough for me to say to myself, *Mate, this is not fully resolved. We need to look at this again.* For all of this I had the support of my psychotherapist, Ernst, and with his help the therapeutic benefits of writing were much more complete and safe.

To benefit from journaling, you don't have to be a scholar. It's not about impressing anyone or getting published (although that may be possible). It's about making sense of and processing your own experience. Your truth.

CHAPTER 18

Reflections

In Part 1, I shared what it was like for me living with PTSD and depression and discussed stress and burnout. I also gave personal insights into the topic of suicide. In Part 2 I shared my recovery journey, including the importance of my recovery game plan and the strategies I used in that plan to get well. I also introduced the 'rings of recovery' and discussed the elements of a good recovery framework. Last of all, in Part 3 I shared how I not only recovered my mental health but have also used what I learned through that journey to help navigate significant life challenges and adversities since. Collectively, what I have shared in this book is a story of *post-traumatic growth*, which I will talk about shortly, but before I do, there is one point I'd like to make.

It is not my wish to leave you with the impression that I think I have life all worked out and am living trouble-free. Far from it. I have perfectionist personality traits and character flaws that I am always trying to work on, and like everyone, I make my fair share of mistakes. My post-pandemic business recovery provides a great example.

It took three years for Mentality Plus to return to pre-pandemic business levels, and when it happened, I made a commitment to myself that I would not get caught in the trap of trying to make up for lost time and income. Unfortunately, though, at a subconscious level at least, that's exactly what I did. I got so caught up in the excitement of bouncing back, especially with the new programs I had developed, that I lost the ability and discipline to say no. Spaces in my calendar that I normally reserve for recharging I filled with more work, and I ignored all the classic warning signs of looming burnout. By the time Christmas arrived and I finally stopped, it all washed over me and I was in a bit of trouble. But thankfully, this time it wasn't a knockout blow but more a clip across the jaw as a warning shot.

The day after Boxing Day I rose before dawn, sat down in my office, pulled out a notepad and pen and got to work on another recovery game plan. I put up my scaffolding. Once again, alcohol and caffeine were the first to go, and I renewed my commitment to meditation, exercise and gratitude journaling. I also took time away from writing this book, removed myself from all sources of media news, booked in some therapy sessions with Ernst, and simply allowed myself to rest. Because I backed away from the cliff edge of burnout before I stepped off, it only took a month to get myself levelled out. By the time I started taking bookings for the new year, I was recharged and ready for work, but this time far more mindful of prioritising self-care above all else.

I guess what I am trying to say is this. I have come a long way since my breakdown in 2012, and after everything I have been through since, there is not much that really shakes me. However, I am flesh and blood and just as human as everyone else, and like everyone else, I don't always get things right. As much as I can be a perfectionist at times, I am far from perfect. But one strength I possess that I have built on over the years is a deep sense of self-awareness. Self-awareness is my compass. And like any compass, when I stray off course, by taking the time to stop, think and make corrections, I always get myself heading back in the right direction. Recovery isn't about getting to a point of living a perfect life – it's about living the best life I can, and having someone special to share it with has helped.

■ ■ ■

In 2020, at the beginning of the pandemic, I met and fell in love with Kyla. I wasn't looking and she wasn't looking, so it was totally unexpected, which made it even more special.

I have talked about the benefits of finding things

to be grateful for in the challenges and adversities we face in life, and Kyla is a perfect example. If I have one thing for which to be grateful in all the loss and hurt experienced by me and my family because of divorce, it is definitely Kyla. Because we both left our previous relationships carrying no burden of anger, bitterness or resentment, our hearts and minds were free for us to find each other and fully enjoy the journey. We live in our own home now at Lake Macquarie with Kyla's young teenage kids, Morgan and Eartha, and our dog, Molly. It is a home full of love.

My three sons have grown up and made their own way in life, and I am proud of all of them. My eldest, Hughie, married during the pandemic and soon after became a dad, and I became a pop. Becoming a pop to my granddaughter, Thea, has been one of the most beautiful experiences of my life. It completes me. After Thea was born, I sat with Hughie one afternoon in my dining room and shared with him the challenge I made to myself to try to be a better dad than the one I had, and that when the time came, I would offer that same challenge to each of my sons. He is already a great dad, but still, I think he liked the idea.

■ ■ ■

One of the reasons I moved back to Newcastle after my marital separation was having an established network of lifelong friends, and together, they were the foundation stone on which I rebuilt my life. No matter how much my police career and the tyranny of distance caused me to drift away, my core group of mates from high school have never given up on me and have always been there when I needed them. My mates and I have history: we know each other like no one else can, we never judge each other, we are there for each other with support when needed, and no one makes me laugh like those boys do.

Just recently I heard a song that reminded me of one of my first detective partners in the early 1990s. Dick often picked me up in his red sports car, and we would travel to work with his favourite, Frankie Valli and the Four Seasons, blaring through the stereo speakers. I enjoyed the memory so much that I sent out a simple text to him, sharing the experience and what it meant to me, and then he got to enjoy the memory as well, and now we have arranged to catch up in person. Staying connected or reconnecting with friends and maintaining healthy social networks is one of the best things we can do for our mental health and wellbeing. I cherish mine.

■ ■ ■

I first heard the term *post-traumatic growth* during a wellbeing program delivered by psychotherapist Margie Braunstein from the Quest for Life Foundation, and I was immediately drawn to it. First developed by psychologists Richard Tedeschi and Lawrence Calhoun in the 1990s, it explains the ability of people to achieve positive psychological change as a direct result of facing trauma and hardship. I think I was drawn to the expression because I identify with it, as do many others.

My dear friend Esther McKay, a former police forensic investigator, has for the last twenty years used her experience of living with PTSD to help others. In 2005, Esther, Bob Walsh and Suzana Whybro established the Police Post Trauma Support Group, a first of its kind, to help current and former police officers and their families cope with and recover from the challenges of trauma-related mental health problems. The peer support group became a registered charity and grew to have branches established all over New South Wales. Together they have helped thousands of police and their families navigate the hardships of PTSD. Esther was also a pioneer of police and true crime memoir with two bestselling books that brought the hardships of first-responder roles to the attention of the wider public. I have had the pleasure of working with her at Backup for Life and with the Quest for Life Foundation at Bundanoon. Esther is living the example of post-traumatic growth.

Back in 1994 I met two wonderful people in the worst possible circumstances. Ron and Narelle Lockhart's young son Andrew was senselessly murdered on the main street of Hay in outback New South Wales, and at twenty-four years of age, I was the detective in charge of the investigation.

There is nothing I have seen that compares to the level of grief and loss associated with homicide, but to their credit, Ron and Narelle refused to allow themselves to become helpless victims. They joined other courageous parents at the newly formed Homicide Victims Support Group (HVSG), and after the conviction of their son's killers, they set about supporting other families visited by the trauma of homicide, often sitting with them in court through entire criminal trials. With Narelle in support, Ron has devoted his life to the HVSG, and their surviving son, Graham, became a police officer. Sadly, over four thousand families have joined HSVG since 1994, but in using their own devastating experience to rise up and help others, the Lockhart family truly define post-traumatic growth.

I am amazed at how life sometimes finds a way to bring people together. Shortly after moving to my second unit complex in Swan Bay at Lake Macquarie, Danny Jeffery moved into the villa next door. Danny was recently divorced like me, and where I was a twenty-five-year veteran of the police force, Danny was a thirty-five-year veteran of the Australian Defence Force. During eighty-five ground combat missions in Afghanistan, Danny accumulated significant physical injuries, but eventually it was psychological injuries that not only ended his career but also very nearly his life. Danny refused to give up on his recovery. He turned to adaptive sport, competing in the Orlando and Toronto Invictus Games in 2016 and 2017 before becoming an Australian coach for the 2018 games in Sydney. He joined the wheelchair tennis international professional circuit and attained a ranking in the top 150 before his long list of military injuries forced retirement. Danny has recovered from PTSD, major depressive disorder and anxiety disorder and is now using his experience as a suicide survivor in hospital emergency department peer support work specialising in suicide prevention. In using his lived experiences to give back to others, Danny has turned a negative to a positive, loss into gain, and has come out the other side stronger. He has experienced post-traumatic growth.

The reason I have shared the three stories above is that, like me, they are not household names. Most people have not heard of Esther McKay, or Ron and Narelle Lockhart, or Danny Jeffery, but these are people who I know serve as extraordinary examples of post-traumatic growth. They have all lifted themselves above their traumas and adversity and then turned those negative experiences into something positive for the benefit of others. I could easily fill a book with the stories of many others I know who have achieved similar post-traumatic growth. Life is tough, and there is no avoiding hardship. But trauma, adversity and mental health problems do not have to negatively define us as victims. Like the three wonderful examples above, and sometimes with a little help along the way, all of us have the capacity to take back control, recover and *grow* through life's challenges.

■■■

In late 2022, I travelled to Sydney and delivered a talk to a men's support group. It was an informal affair, about thirty men gathered on sofas and benches at an inner-city brewery. Before the event concluded, one bloke put up his hand and asked me a last question.

'Craig, you've shared with us some of the mistakes you made and the consequences, but I'm wondering, if you could go back in time and change anything, would you?'

It was a great question, and I took a moment before finally answering, 'No, mate, I wouldn't.' And then I explained why.

First, I have made plenty of mistakes in my life. Some of those mistakes have hurt those closest to me. Some of those mistakes ended a career I loved. But I have played life the best I can with the cards I was dealt, and I have made a choice. That choice is not to live with regret. Life is way too short for living under the heavy burden of regret. Instead, I choose to accept my mistakes, learn from them, and strive to be the best Craig that I can be. Second, everything that I've done in my life, the good and the bad, and all the challenges I've faced have shaped me into the man I am now, and I'm proud to be that man. I wouldn't change a thing. And to finish, I'd like to share this short example of the power of perspective.

A good friend of mine and my psychotherapist, Ernst Meyer, once said to me in session, 'Craig, when you are talking, I often hear you referring to the event of your mental breakdown. Could I suggest to you an alternative?'

'Sure, Ernst,' I said.

'Do you think your breakdown could be better described as your *breakthrough*?'

Absolutely it could be.

And I am now all the more grateful for it.

Acknowledgements

As I continue to discover, there is much hard work and collaboration from many for books like mine to ever reach the hands of you, the reader. This one started as an idea, but became a reality with the support, advice and guidance of the following people.

The Echo Publishing team. Emily in marketing and publicity, publishing manager Diana Hill and managing director Juliet Rogers. All of you have worked incredibly hard to make this happen and as always, I felt safe with my manuscript in your hands. Thank you for making me feel part of the family.

Josh Durham of Design by Committee. Thank you once again for capturing my message in your wonderful cover design.

Editor Simone Ford. As a writer, from you I have learned so much, and for catching my errors, tightening structure and providing sound, objective advice once again, I am very grateful.

Ernst Meyer, Psychotherapist. Thank you for your wise counsel and for helping me unpack and debrief the many issues raised during my writing of this book.

Margie Braunstein, Psychotherapist. I have learned a lot from you over the years we have worked together. Thanks for opening my mind to so much.

My dear friend and colleague, Trev Walter. Every time I strap on my helmet, jump on the saddle and open the throttle, you're there with me now, mate. The world was so much richer for you being in it and remains so in your memory.

My mum, Wendy. As always, I value your support and advice. Thanks for being in my corner.

My sons Hugh, Owen and Niam. For being there for me through the thick of it, and still being there on the other side, thank you. I am proud of you all and I love you very much.

Eartha and Morgan. For morning after morning trying so hard to be quiet when I'm in my office writing, but also for being such a big part of my life, thank you both.

Kyla. The flame just keeps burning brighter and brighter. For your patience, for caring, for listening and for loving me so much, I thank you with all my heart. With you, I am truly home.

And last of all ...

For all the hundreds of people I have been fortunate to meet, who have shared with me their own mental health challenges and life adversities, and in doing so deepened my own understanding of life, you have my sincere thanks, gratitude and very best wishes.